A CAREER IN LANGUAGE TRANSLATION

Insightful information to guide you in your journey as a professional translator

Carline Férailleur-Dumoulin

authorHOUSE®

AuthorHouse™
1663 Liberty Drive, Suite 200
Bloomington, IN 47403
www.authorhouse.com
Phone: 1-800-839-8640

First published by AuthorHouse 5/8/2009

ISBN: 978-1-4389-4422-7 (sc)
ISBN: 978-1-4389-4423-4 (hc)

Library of Congress Control Number: 2009901616

Printed in the United States of America
Bloomington, Indiana
This book is printed on acid-free paper.

TABLE OF CONTENTS

PREFACE

The simple fact that you are holding this book in your hands is an indication of your interest in the field of language translation. Whether you are new to the field, a college student taking translation course, a graduate student, a working professional translator or linguist, a faculty member, regardless of your current status in the field of translation, you will most certainly find the information in this book useful and of great help to you in your journey in the translation field.

My goal in writing this book is to provide you with a guide. It is a compilation of years of research and experience as a freelance translator as well as experience as a translation business owner. I only hope that you will greatly benefit from it and perhaps avoid some of the mistakes I made when I started in this business.

The main focus in this book will be translation; even though there will be some mentions of interpretation. Also, I will briefly cover the aspect of running a translation company. This will at least allow you to have a general idea of what is involved in running a translation company. And should you decide to pursue that route, I suggest you look at additional resources that provide greater details on running a small business. Throughout the book, you will notice some terms in bold, please refer to the glossary on the back for a clear definition of the term in question. I've only bolded the first occurrence of the term referenced in the glossary.

I hope you enjoy this book as much as I have enjoyed writing it. Best of Luck to you as you embark on your Translation career!

Sincerely,

Carline Férailleur-Dumoulin

Acknowledgments

So many people have contributed, in many ways, to the completion of this book.

I would like to thank AuthorHouse and its team of wonderful professionals, for publishing this book. A special thank you to Becca Zupann, Publishing Consultant, Anthony Schrock, Marketing Consultant, and Erin McAuley, Design Consultant. You have really guided me and counseled me during the initial stages of this project.

A special thanks to my mentors and professors at New York University, School of Continuing Studies, for providing me with the necessary tools and knowledge that have allowed me to become the professional translator that I am today.

As in anything in life, everyday is an opportunity for learning and new challenges. I am thankful to all of my colleagues and friends in the field who have collaborated with me on multiple projects. It goes without saying that I am very grateful to all of my loyal clients, who have provided me with the opportunity to work on endless projects.

I would like to thank Jeff Sanfacon, the Editor of the ATA Chronicle, for the permission to reproduce the quotations found in this book.

To my closest and dearest: words alone cannot express my gratitude. All of you have always been there to guide me, to support me and to encourage me in all of my endeavors. Thank you to my wonderful parents for the continued support and encouragement. Thank you to my dear sister and best friend, Nancy, for not only having edited this work, but also for all the feedback and much needed assistance during the creation of this book. To my precious son P.C., the source and inspiration for this book. Last but certainly not least, to my wonderful soulmate, my other half, my best friend, my guide, my voice of reason, my husband, Philippe. Thank you for having shared with me your expertise in the field; for your never-ending support and for having encouraged me to go through with this project. Thank you for all of your valuable input and thank you for your much needed patience.

Carline

CHAPTER 1
INTRODUCTION

Translation involves more than the conversion of text from one language into another. As a translator and/or interpreter, our role is to facilitate the cross-cultural communication that is needed in our world today. In addition to converting words or text, we transmit concepts and ideas from one language into another. A translator or interpreter, must fully understand the subject matter in which he or she works, in order to accurately convey the information. At times, translation involves research. Words or expressions evolve over time. And also, new words or expressions are created from generation to generation. As a translator or interpreter, we must familiarize ourselves with the current trends and expressions being used so that our translation accurately reflects the actual cultural meaning in the target language.

Translation is usually charged per word or character. Occasionally, translation is charged per page, usually when the document is voluminous and the manual count of the hard copies would take too long; it can also be charged by the hour (generally this hourly rate applies to **proofreading** and **editing**); sometimes too the charge is per document (for example, most translators charge a flat rate for standard birth, marriage and death certificates and school diplomas).

A translator or interpreter must be fluent in at least two languages; their **native language** and a secondary language; some translators and interpreters are fluent in more than two languages. Their native language, sometimes referred to as their active language, is the primary or first language they learned since early childhood and this is the language they translate into (**target language**). Their secondary language, also referred to as their passive

1

language (**source language**), is one they must have excellent knowledge of. Translators who are **near-native** speakers of a language, in other words, who have mastered both the language and its sociocultural norms at a native speaker's level translate from and into both languages, their native language and their near-native language.

Even though the words translation and interpretation are used interchangeably, there is a significant difference between the two. As a professional, you must be aware of that difference and recognize which one you have the expertise in. Translation is the conversion of *written* text from one language into another. As a translator, you must have excellent writing and analytical skills. You must also have good editing and proofreading skills.

On the other hand, interpretation involves the conversion of one *spoken* language into another. This means that a good interpreter must pay careful attention to what is being said, he or she must understand the subject matter being communicated, and must be able to clearly express the thoughts and ideas needed to be conveyed. Strong memory skills, analytical skills and communication skills are required.

Nowadays, most translation work is done on a computer. Most assignments are sent electronically. This allows translators to work from anywhere, as long as they have access to a computer and their reference materials. You will find that most translators work from home, for the most part.

THE HISTORY OF TRANSLATION

The word translation, comes from the Latin word "translatio" derived from the perfect passive participle of "translatum" or "transferre", which means "to transfer" – from "trans" meaning "across" plus "ferre" which means "to carry" or "to bring".[1]

Translation has played an important role in history. We can somewhat trace back the history of translation to Bible Translation. Budhist monks translated the Indian Sutras (scriptures containing the teachings of Buddha) into Chinese and adapted these translations to reflect China's varied culture.[1]

One of the famous mistranslation of the Bible is the translation of the Hebrew word "*keren*", translated as "horn" in a context where it should have been translated as "beam of light". As a result, for centuries, artists have depicted Moses the Lawgiver with horns growing out of his forehead. An example is portrayed in Michelangelo's famous sculpture of Moses.[1]

In the West, one of the early recordings of translation was that of the *Septuagint,* which is the Greek translation of the Jewish Scriptures in Hebrew, during the third century B.C.E. The term *Septuagint* refers to the "seventy" Jewish scholars (according to some versions, there were seventy-two scholars) who were commissioned in Alexandria, during the reign of Ptolemy Philadelphus to carry out the task of translation. The *Septuagint* was the source of the Old Testament for early Christians.[3]

Saint Jerome, the patron of translators, is still considered one of the greatest translators of all time for having translated the Bible into Latin.[1]

Translation of the Bible into local European languages took place right before and during the Protestant Reformation. This movement had a major impact on Western Christianity's split into Roman Catholicism and Protestantism, because of the disparities that existed in the Catholic and Protestant versions of the words and passages.[1]

The Bible was translated from Latin into English only during the fourteenth century, by John Wycliffe, John Purvey and Nicholas of Hereford. They created two editions of the Wycliffe Bible. Back then, Latin was the dominant language in the western church.[1,2]

Also during the fourteenth century, other translation works were found in poetry. The first great translations into English were made by the English poet Geoffrey Chaucer, whose first best known work is *The Canterbury Tales.* Chaucer adapted *Knight's Tale,* one of the twenty-two completed Canterbury Tales, from the Italian version of *Teseida* by Giovanni Boccacio[5]. In addition, his work *Troilus and Criseyde* was also adapted from Boccaccio's Italian version of *Il Filostrato*[6]. He also began a translation of the French version of *Roman de La Rose* written by Guillaume de Lorris and Jean de Meun; and completed the translation of the Latin version of *The Consolation of Philosophy by* Boethius[4].

ACADEMIC EDUCATION AND TRAINING

If you are interested in pursuing a career in translation, the best way to start is by making sure you are fluent in at least two languages. Then, start by taking relevant courses in your active and passive languages. It is imperative to take some writing classes, in both languages, if you have not done so already. Pursue a Degree or Certificate in Translation. Contact your local college or university to see if they offer such program. If it's not available, look for online programs offered by other institutions. Please refer to Appendix E for a partial list of Institutions offering a program in Translation and/or Interpretation in the United States and Abroad. Exchange programs are also a good way to familiarize yourself with the culture and to improve your language skills.

Whenever you get a chance, travel to foreign countries, mainly countries where the foreign language you will translate from is spoken. Familiarize yourself with their culture and customs, the latest neologism (actually in both languages). Speak to people from your country of interest. Read books. Do online research. Don't hesitate to ask questions.

To acquire some experience and in order to gain entry into the field, you might want to consider doing pro-bono translation work; make sure you establish a good relationship with those clients and use them as your professional references.

Use your existing skills and field experience to your advantage. For example, if you have experience in the banking sector, and now want to pursue a translation career, it is a great idea to specialize in financial translation. Of course, you should still pursue an academic training in translation for that specialization but you have a great chance of excelling in this area since you have field experience.

TRANSLATORS' CERTIFICATION AND ACCREDITATION

In the above section, I mentioned pursuing an academic training in Translation. In addition to pursuing an academic training and receiving a degree in translation and/or interpretation through an academic institution, translators and interpreters can obtain certification through recognized professional organizations and through the government. To date, the United States, unlike some other countries, does not have a federal or state licensing or certification program for translators.

Today, the most widely accepted form of Translator's Certification in the United States is through the **American Translators Association,** commonly referred to as **ATA.**

The American Translators Association (ATA) is a professional association, founded in 1959, to advance the translation and interpreting professions and foster the professional development of individual translators and interpreters. Its 10,000 members in more than 90 countries include translators, interpreters, teachers, project managers, web and software developers, language company owners, hospitals, universities, and government agencies. Association membership is available to individuals (Active, Corresponding, Associate, Student) and organizations (Corporate, Institutional).

In order to be an ATA-Certified Translator, you must be an ATA member. Membership also allows you to purchase practice tests, which will give you an insight on the nature of the examination and on how the evaluators grade the tests. This also is a good way for you to determine how well-prepared you are to take the actual exam, since your practice test will be graded by ATA graders. Furthermore, to take the actual examination, you must satisfy ATA's eligibility requirements and to maintain certification credential, the translator must complete an ethics workshop or course within the first three-year period after certification, in addition to completing at least 20 hours of continuing education credits through coursework, seminars and conferences. You have to provide proof of a combination of education and work experience. Then, you have to register to take the examination, which is a three-hour, open-book, proctored exam. As of April 2008, the ATA offered Certification in 26 language pairs.

For full details on the ATA-Certification Exam, please visit their website at **www.atanet.org** or contact them at (703) 683-6100.

The National Association of Judiciary Interpreters and Translators (NAJIT) is a professional association that was first chartered as a non-profit organization under the New York State Laws and was incorporated as the Court Interpreters and Translators Association, Inc. (CITA) in 1978. NAJIT seeks to promote quality interpretation and translation within the judicial system. It has over 1200 members including practicing interpreters, translators, educators, researchers, students and administrators. Most of its members are located in the United States; however, it has members in Latin America, in Europe, in Asia and in Australia.

NAJIT offers a certification credential, referred to as the Nationally Certified Judiciary Interpreter and Translator or NCJIT. Achieving this NCJIT credential demonstrates an individual's commitment to upholding the highest standards in the profession. The NCJIT credential is awarded to those individuals who pass a rigorous examination of overall language skills and the common body of knowledge relevant to the judiciary and related areas, and who have shown an understanding of and willingness to comply with a professional Code of Ethics and Professional Responsibilities.

The NCJIT examination is the only nationwide certification exam developed exclusively by judiciary interpreters and translators. Its purpose is to create a uniform standard for interpreters and translators working in a wide variety of legal settings, both civil and penal, throughout the United States. It is the first examination that tests both interpreting and translation skills in a legal setting. It is the only examination that confers a credential offered by the profession, which belongs to the individual regardless of employment status or geographic location. As of the date of publication of this book, this examination was being offered in Spanish only. NAJIT is working on developing the NCJIT in other languages as well.

The NCJIT examination consists of a written component and an oral component. Candidates must pass the written examination before they can be eligible to take the oral examination. In order to maintain certification credential, individuals must accumulate 30 Continuing Education Credits (CEU's) every three years, effective on the date certification is obtained or effective on the date of the last recertification.

For full details on NAJIT membership and their Certification credential, please visit their website at www.najit.org or contact them at (202) 293-0342.

Washington State Department of Social and Health Services (DSHS)

In 1991, the Department of Social and Health Services (DSHS) in Washington State initiated an effort to certify medical and social service interpreters and translators working for DSHS throughout its many divisions and programs. This included the Medical Assistance Administration and, therefore, interpreters for Medicaid patients. This effort was the culmination of lawsuits and civil rights complaints brought against DSHS for not providing equal access to services for Limited English Proficient (LEP) clients. As part of a consent decree, DSHS agreed not only to provide (and pay for) interpreters for clients, but also to ensure the quality of interpreter services provided. DSHS chose to ensure quality through the development and administration of a standardized test.

The Language Testing and Certification program (LTC) was created to develop systems, methods, procedures, and policies in carrying out the department's commitment.

The tests developed by LTC aim to measure both language proficiency in English and a second language as well as interpreting/translation skills. DSHS language certification is currently available in eight languages: Spanish, Vietnamese, Russian, Cambodian, Laotian, Mandarin Chinese, Cantonese Chinese, and Korean. Qualification screening tests are also available in all other languages.

The Language Testing and Certification (LTC) program provides the following services:

1) Language proficiency testing and certification/authorization of DSHS bilingual employees, applicants for bilingual positions, contracted interpreters, contracted translators, and licensed agency personnel. 2) Providing consultation to the department in establishing DSHS policies regarding the quality of language services to Limited English Proficient (LEP) clients. 3) Managing the roster of certified interpreters and translators; managing the roster of authorized interpreters.

Translators and Interpreters must be able to serve DSHS clients in Washington State in order to be considered for the LTC and for possible employment.

For more information about Washington State Department of Social and Health Services (DSHS), please visit their website at www1.dshs.wa.gov.

For information about the Language Testing and Certification (LTC) program, visit their direct link at www1.dshs.wa.gov/msa/ltc.

You may call them at (360) 664-6035 for more information about their certification program; or call them at (800) 605-5126 for general information.

United Nations Language Proficiency Examinations (LPE)

The Language Proficiency Examination is used by the United Nations to test the written and spoken knowledge of staff members in the six official languages of the United Nations: Arabic, Chinese, English, French, Russian and Spanish.

Adequate and demonstrated knowledge in one of these official languages will be established by means of a language proficiency certificate awarded by the United Nations upon the staff member's successfully passing the United Nations Language Proficiency Examination (LPE) in that language. Staff members who pass one or more examination(s) qualify for language related incentives. The LPE consists of a written part and an oral part, which are to be taken at the same session. A minimum score of 65 percent in both parts is required for a passing grade.

The Oral Part of the Language Proficiency Examination consists of an interview of up to 15 minutes long, conducted by an interviewer. The purpose of the oral part is to obtain a sample of the candidate's linguistic competence in the language being tested.

The Written Part of the Language Proficiency Examination is administered in a single session lasting 3 hours and 10 minutes. The written part consists of a composition and a series of multiple-choice questions covering listening comprehension, reading comprehension, vocabulary and grammar.

To be eligible for LPE, the following requirements must be met:

Individuals who have participated in a United Nations language course and who have completed the highest level of that course are required to pass the final exam at the highest level of the United Nations Language and Communications Program.

Staff members who have studied a language outside the United Nations or regularly use it at work, home, or school must have at least 2 years of practice in the language they want to be tested in. The decision on eligibility is made on a case to case basis. For that purpose, candidates must provide full details of his/her language training (i.e., name of institution, courses, dates, length of study) on the LPE Registration form (as provided for on the LPE application form and submit the written statement along with the application form).

Staff members from United Nations or affiliated agencies serving on fixed term or permanent contracts, are eligible to take the LPE provided that their contract expiration date is after the date of the LPE.

Staff members, including those serving on short-term appointments, whose contracts expire before the date of the LPE, must obtain authorization from their executive officer or head of administration, as provided for on the LPE application form and submit it along with the registration form.

You are also able to obtain practice exams that will help you prepare for the actual examination.

For more information about this program, visit http://www.un.org/exam/lpe. You may also call them at (917) 367-8018 or (212) 963-0086.

COURT INTERPRETERS' CERTIFICATION AND REGISTRATION

Interpreters wishing to be certified or registered through the Court system must contact the Administrative Office of the Courts in their State to inquire about the specific requirements for certification and/or registration.

Certification is the highest level of formal accreditation an Interpreter is able to obtain.

I must note that not all States offer Certification to their Court Interpreters. Some may offer the Certification Exam, however, examination in the candidate's language pair may not be offered. Generally, in order for an interpreter to be a **certified interpreter**, the candidate must pass the Court Interpreter Certification Examination, complete an Interpreter's Orientation Workshop, pass a written exam in English, which covers a section on Ethics, take and pass the Oral Proficiency Interview (OPI) and execute the Oath of Interpreter.

Interpreters of spoken languages for which there is no state-certifying examination are required to pass the English Fluency Examination and fulfill the corresponding Judicial Council requirements in order to become a **registered interpreter** of a nondesignated language. To become a registered interpreter, the candidate must complete the Court Interpreter Orientation Workshop, take and pass the written test, administered in English, and take the **Oral Proficiency Interview (OPI)**.

Court Interpreters must adhere to the Code of Professional Responsibility for Court Interpreters.

Contact the Administrative Office of the Courts in your State in order to obtain requirements that are specific to your particular State.

CAREER OPPORTUNITIES

A translation career can be a very lucrative one. The industry is a very fragmented industry. There are few large companies; many medium ones and small ones generating less than $500,000 in annual sales; the very small companies are comprised of freelancers who've incorporated and run their companies alone. Among some of the very large companies, Lionbridge, founded in 1996 and with its headquarters located in Waltham, Massachusetts, is recognized as the largest translation and localization company in the world. This company reported a total revenue of $452 Million dollars for the 2007 Fiscal Year. It is also publicly traded. In the United States, Eriksen Translations, Inc, located in Brooklyn, New York reported annual sales of over $4 Million dollars for the 2007 Fiscal Year, based on a report by Dun and Bradstreet. In addition, Cyracom International, based in Tucson Arizona and specializing in healthcare and localization, as well as ETranslate, acquired by translations.com and providing globalization technology and services for the Fortune 1000 companies, can also be considered among the large translation companies. Transperfect, headquartered in New York City has over 50 offices in 4 continents. Can Talk (Canada) Inc., founded by Maureen Mitchell, focuses on providing customized services, high quality, immediate and rapid response language services supported by unique service delivery applications. Argos Company Ltd is one of the largest translations and globalization companies in Eastern Europe. It is an American-British owned company, specializing in Central and Eastern European support. Their headquarters is in Krakow, Poland and their regional office, Argos Translations Inc. is located in Chicago Illinois.

A freelance translator has great potential to earn revenues as high as $80,000 a year. Of course, this will depend on the high demand for the translator's language pair(s) and field(s) of expertise.

Translation is a booming business. There will always be a need for language translation. Some might argue that human translation will become obsolete and will be replaced by **machine translation**. It is highly unlikely.

Machine translation cannot provide culturally-adapted translation that us humans we provide.

A career in translation or interpretation offers a bright future. The U.S. Department of Labor reports, "Employment of interpreters and translators is projected to increase 24 percent over the 2006-16 decade, much faster than the average for all occupations. This growth will be driven partly by strong demand in health care settings and work related to homeland security."[A]

Interpreters and translators work in a variety of industries. Some work in public and private educational institutions, and a good number work in health care and social administration. Others work in the government sector, at the Federal, State and local levels. Some translators and interpreters who are freelancers, work part-time and rely on other sources of income as their main income.

The employment outlook for translators and interpreters is pretty strong. Recent government policies and legislation in support of Title VI of the Civil Rights Act have created a greater demand for translators and interpreters in healthcare and government agencies. On August 11, 2000, President Bill Clinton signed Executive Order 13166, "Improving Access to Services for Persons with Limited English Proficiency" which is an enforcement of Title VI of the Civil Rights Act of 1964. The objective of this order is to "improve access to federally conducted and federally assisted programs and activities for persons, who as a result of national origin, are limited in their English proficiency (LEP)".[B]

Areas of Specialization

The following is a partial list of areas of translation specialization: medical, legal, literary, technical, business, automotive, banking, finance, marketing, civil and mechanical engineering, advertising, academia, website, general. And there is now a great need for **localization** translation. It involves the complete adaptation of a product or service to a particular language culture. A common example is software localization.

As a translator, it's best to specialize in more than one area of expertise. This increases your chances of finding frequent work. In addition, a broad knowledge in various areas is very helpful.

CHAPTER 2
GETTING STARTED

Auto-Analysis and Assessment

What should you do to get started?

First and foremost, you must ask yourself the following questions:

Why do I want to enter into this profession? Do I have a passion for languages? What are my qualifications? What area(s) do I want to specialize in? Do I want to be a freelancer? Do I want to work full time or part time? Do I want to work for a translation company, as an in-house translator, and maybe as a **Project Manager**? Do I want to work for an international organization? Do I want to work for the Federal Government? Do I want to run my own translation company? How big do I want my translation company to be? How much money do I want to make? What is my goal? What are my strengths and weaknesses? Who are my competitors?

You must ask yourself all of the above questions in order to decide if this is the right profession for you.

Let me share some critical points to keep in mind when making your decision. If you decide to be a freelancer, know that as a freelancer, you will have no benefits, no 401K, no health insurance, no paid vacations. You will be responsible for paying your taxes for the previous fiscal year that you worked as a freelancer. There will be no deductions from your pay for tax provision. Whatever amount you negotiate upfront with your client, that's the amount you will receive as your payment for performing an assignment. More often than not, payment for translation and/or interpreting assignments are made on a **net 30** or **net 45** basis. In other words, you will receive your payment 30 to 45 days after you've submitted your invoice for the assignment. You have to be determined and market yourself continously to find work. Basically, you are on your own!

NECESSARY SKILLS

As a professional translator, you must be able to work under tight deadlines and deliver the translation on time. It is also important for you to know your limits, in terms of subject matter, work capacity, and project delivery schedule.

A professional translator must possess good typing and translation speed. It is also important for the professional translator to be proficient in word processing. Furthermore, the professional translator needs a working knowledge of hardware, software and should be able to browse the Internet with ease. There will be times when you will need to do extensive research on a specific subject, and being able to browse the Internet with no problem, will prove to be beneficial.

The good way to pick up typing and translation speed is with practice. On your free time, pick up a text (from a book, newspaper article, or even a business correspondence) and translate it into your native language. This is a good way to gain experience, pick up speed and familiarize yourself with different subject matter. As you do these practice exercises, be sure to build a glossary, according to the subject matter. This will come in very handy. You can also buy typing programs (Mavis Beacon is a good one, for example) that will allow you to pick up speed and evaluate your typing skills along with providing you with your word output based on simulated assessments.

A professional translator must always work on improving his or her language skills and constantly be updated on his or her subject area(s).

USEFUL MATERIALS

A professional translator must be equipped with the right monolingual and bilingual dictionaries, reference materials, thesauri, dictionaries of synonyms, specialized dictionaries, CD-Rom monolingual, bilingual or specialized (optional). I highly recommend having an unabridged dictionary version as part of your dictionary collection. A professional translator must also be familiar with the various online resources available to him or her. There are many terminology databases, dictionaries that are available on the Internet. It's a good idea to research for those online resources and to ask your colleagues to provide you with some of their commonly used weblinks.

SOFTWARE PROGRAMS

In terms of software programs, having a good word processing program and **Computer Aided Translation Tools** (**CAT tools**) is essential.

Spell Checkers

A spell checker is an electronic dictionary built into a word processing program and whose function is to check the spelling of the words found in a document against the proper spellings in the built-in dictionary. The spell checker also provides suggested words as replacements for either an unrecognized word or a misspelled word.

Working with a Spell Checker is very useful. However, you should not simply rely on your Spell Checker as a way to confirm that your text is free from grammatical error. You should have a good idea on how Spell Checkers work. For example, see the sentence below. I ran it through my Spell Checker while writing this book, on my Word 2003 program. The only error found was the word "chequer" for which it provided a few suggested replacements, none of which were the right spelling of the word, "checker".

"Eye am going to run this sentence threw this spell chequer two see if it will catch sum of the errors found in this sentence."

That said, after running your spell check, be sure to proofread your document in its entirety to avoid a similar scenario as mentioned above. This spell checker obviously does not have the capacity to detect context, that is why those misspelled words were overlooked. According to the spell checker and the dictionary, the word "eye", for example, is spelled correctly. Yet, not in this particular sentence.

Translation Memory

A **Translation Memory** software or **TM**, is a database which stores sentences and their translations for use in future translations.

The way a translation memory software works is as follows: As the translator types in the translation of the source document, the TM stores the translated source texts along with their corresponding target texts in a database and retrieves related segments, or manageable source text units, during the translation of new texts. As the translator continues with the translation of the document, the TM searches for a matching source segment that was previously stored in its database, displays that source segment and provides a previously stored translation. At that point, the translator can either accept the suggested translation, replace it with a new translation, or change it to match the source. If there is no matching segment in the TM's database, the software, then allows the translator to enter a translation for the new segment; and this time it stores it into its database for future use. Some translation memory systems search for what is referred to as 100% matches only, which means they can only retrieve segments of text that match entries in the database word for word; while there are other TM's, that use a process called fuzzy matching to retrieve similar segments. Fuzzy matching or fuzzy match is an approximate match of the entries in the database; they are usually represented in percentages. Translation memory software search for text in the source segment. They work best on texts which are highly repetitive. However, when a translator uses a TM overtime this can definitely save the translator considerable amount of time and work.

There are many benefits associated with working with a Translation Memory software. For one, when a translator works with a TM, this is one way of ensuring the entire document is translated, because as you work on the document, the TM does not allow you to move on to the next segment until the current segment has been translated. One of the key benefits is that the translated document will be consistent throughout. Another benefit to the translator is speed in the translation process. As the TM provides previously translated texts, the translator does not have to take time to re-translate the repeated source text.

Translation memory software also have their disadvantages, which certainly do not outweigh the benefits. One of the disadvantages is that TM's do not currently support all types of document formats and may not be able to support all file types either.

When using a translation memory software, a translator must be very careful. Special care is called for when the TM is provided by your client.

Even though the TM might show 100% match for a specific source segment, it's always best to read and compare the source text with the matched text provided by the TM if using this TM for the first time. The reason why I say this is because, if you are working with a different type of file, you need to be very careful in ensuring that the context and message being conveyed in the source text is the exact same as the translation provided by the TM. As we know, the same word, or even the same sentence can have different meanings depending on the context, and thus may require a different translation. Once you start to become familiar with the TM and the text, there will be no need for you to review each segment provided by the translation memory software. The only time I recommend you continue to review those segments is when you are not the one who originally created the TM. What you must keep in mind is that the TM provides you with the translation that was entered by a human being; in other words, if there is an error in the translation, it will be reflected in the TM; and guess what? as a professional translator, you are responsible for the translation you provide, therefore it is your responsibility to ensure your translation is accurate. Another not so positive aspect is the cost of a good translation memory software. The cost can vary from $400 U.S. dollars up to over $1,000 U.S. dollars.

Overall, despite the disadvantages we encounter with Translation Memory software, they are still very useful tools for the professional translator. Nowadays, having a TM is practically a must, if you want to be able to work with translation companies and provide fast accurate and up to date service.

Some of the most common types of Translation Memory software used are Déjà Vu (www.atril.com), SDL Trados 2007 (www.translationzone.com), and Wordfast (www.wordfast.net).

Word Count and Other Practical Software

Microsoft Word provides a word count feature found under the Tools menu. This feature not only provides the number of words in your document, but it also provides the number of characters excluding spaces, the number of characters including spaces, the number of lines, pages and paragraphs in your document. The versions prior to the 2007 version, allow you to select in your word count feature, the option to include text in footnotes and endnotes in the total word count. The 2007 MS Word version, has added another useful feature, where you can also opt to include text in textboxes in the word count, for a more accurate word count.

Another software program that you can use to calculate word count in an editable document is the Translation Memory software, *Trados*. In order to do that, you will need to run an analysis on the document or documents for which you need the word count. You will find that option under the Tools menu and by selecting 'Analyse'.

When dealing with some pdf files and non-editable documents, such as certain scanned documents and image files, for example, a great way to obtain a word count is by using an **OCR** program, or an **Optical Character Recognition** software. What is an OCR? Basically, an OCR is a software program that allows you to convert pdf documents, scanned text and images into editable text files.

There are various OCR programs available. Below, I will list a few to facilitate your search. In addition to obtaining the software directly from the websites provided, you might also want to shop around and visit your local office supplies stores.

Abbyy Finereader offers a selection of products tailored for specific tasks.

Abbyy Finereader allows you to transform printed and pdf documents and document images into editable computer files.

Once you have converted your file(s) into and editable file, you will then be able to perform a word count.

For more information about this software and to download a trial version, visit their website at www.abbyy.com.

If you have an editable adobe file, that is not password protected and you would like to run a word count, you can convert the file into an rft file. You do this by opening the file, and 'Save As' type 'Rich Text Format (.rtf)'. Once you have saved it as an rtf file, you can open this file from Word and perform a word count. Remember, in order to use this option, your pdf file must be an editable format. In other words, if it is a scanned document, you will not be able to do so. You must also have the Full Adobe Version (not simply the Adobe Reader) to perform this task.

Omnipage, is an OCR software that converts paper, pdf and digital camera pictures into easily editable files. If you are only looking for a software to manipulate your pdf files, you might want to look into PDF Converter.

It's a software that converts pdf files into fully-formatted documents, forms and spreadsheets. To find out more information about these two software programs and other available products from the same company, visit their website at www.nuance.com.

Practicount and Invoice count text in multiple files of various formats and make invoices. This program counts words, characters with spaces, characters without spaces, lines, pages and generate invoice. Practicount also counts Japanese and Chinese characters. PractiCount can count text in the following formats: Microsoft Word (doc, rtf), Microsoft Excel (xls, csv) , Microsoft PowerPoint (ppt, pps), Corel Word Perfect (wpd), Adobe Acrobat (pdf), Adobe Framemaker (mif), HTML (htm, html, shtml), and others. It also counts words in text boxes, headers, footers, endnotes. Their website address is www.practiline.com. You can also download a 15 day free trial version to evaluate the software.

Any Count produces automatic word counts, character counts, line counts, and page counts for all common file formats. For more information visit their website on www.anycount.com.

ExactSpent is a time tracking software that enables you to calculate the exact time you spent on a particular job. It enables you to create, start, pause and resume timers for multiple jobs. This is a very useful software for assignments charged by the hour. For more information, visit their website at www.exactspent.com.

When purchasing a word count software, be sure to do your research and talk to colleagues in order to get their feedback about the software they use or would recommend. You can actually post your questions, on translators' forums. Another suggestion is to download free trial versions, when possible so you can test the program. You must keep in mind that some Word count software do not count every single text found in a document. For example, some software do not include text in text boxes, in headers and footers and even in graphs, in their total word count. It's always a good idea to request the word count from your client; even though, you should still run your own, but at least you will be able to compare the two and know if there's a major difference between your client's count and your own.

EQUIPMENTS AND ESSENTIAL TOOLS

Magnifying Glass

It is good practice to have a magnifying glass handy. I prefer the ones with the small built-in light. They are very helpful when you have to deal with handwritten documents or typed documents in very small fonts. You will be surprised to see how much information you can read easily with a magnifying glass.

Scanner

In our line of work, you will soon realize that a good and reliable scanner is instrumental in keeping you competitive and efficient in your work.

Fax

Owning a fax is very important for the professional translator. Quite often, our clients prefer to fax us documents or request for translation, and if you do not have a fax, this will make it very hard for you to increase your customer base. If you are not able to buy a fax maching right away, I highly recommend you consider getting an E-Fax number. This is so practical, since you will receive the fax via your email address. The other advantage to having an e-fax is the fact that, if you travel all the time, you are able to receive the e-fax from anywhere, and your client will not have to pay the extra cost. E-fax allows you to get either a local e-fax number or a toll free number. Even when you have your regular fax number, you will certainly benefit from keeping your e-fax, just as a back-up. If you are considering getting an e-fax number, visit www. efax.com for more information about their fax plans.

UPS

If you live in an area where power shortages occur often or even once in a while, it's worth it to invest in a UPS system. UPS is short for *uninterruptible power supply.* This is an equipment that includes a battery whose purpose is to maintain power when there is a power failure. It keeps your computer running for a certain time (from 10 to up to 80 minutes back up run time, depending on the UPS) to allow you to save data and shut down the computer afterwards. Some UPS's have the capacity to hold up to 12 outlets. You can purchase a UPS at one of your local office supply stores.

Phone Line

Make sure you have a dedicated phone line for your business. If you are not able to have a dedicated phone line from the start, be sure the voice message on your answering machine corresponds to the phone number you have listed on your business cards, resumes and other advertising materials, and that it is professional and gives enough details so the caller knows they are contacting a professional translator and/or interpreter. Avoid having background noise in the message. For example, you might have a message that says something like this: "You have reached, Jane at (give number). I am not able to take your call at this time, please leave your name and phone number and I will return your call as soon as possible. If you are calling with an urgent request, please contact me at (give cell phone number or another contact where you can be reached). Thank you for calling."

If you are away on vacation, make sure your voice message mentions it. Also set your e-mail away message so your clients know you are not available. Of course, you want to be sure you let them know ahead of time as well.

High Speed Internet

If you do not have it already, I highly recommend you get High-Speed Internet connection so you won't have any problems or delays receiving electronic work requests.

Don't forget that both your phone service and Internet service are tax-deductible if they are used for business purposes. You have to report them as a business expense. Keep copies of all bills and payments.

Create a separate professional e-mail account for your translation work.

USEFUL INFORMATION

Keep a good and ongoing relationship with your teachers and classmates. You might be surprised to find out they might be the ones to lead you to your first project or job. Or your classmates might become your vendors if you choose to open a company. They might also become your business partners, should you decide to have a partnership.

As you enter the field, be careful not to make too many expenses all at once. Buy the necessary tools and equipments to get you started first. Then, as you start to receive projects and collect payments, allocate an amount for the purchase of other necessary items. Before you know it, you will have a wide array of reference materials and necessary tools to help you in your business.

Have an efficient and organized filing system. Select a day or two during the week to do your filing. It's not fun to have a lot of files accumulated over time that would take days to file. Also keep a computer file and physical file for each client and each of their projects. Make sure your filing cabinets have keys that only you and/or an authorized employee has access to. Remember, you are responsible for maintaining your client's confidentiality. It's important to have hard copy files, just in case your computer crashes! Always back up your work on CDs, external drives, or memory cards. This is very important.

As a professional translator, you must stand by your values. Always keep a professional image. Know how you will answer your phone. Make sure you have a dedicated office space. Make sure there is minimal or no background noise when working (TV, children, dogs, etc.). Return calls and reply to email requests promptly. Even if it's to simply acknowledge receipt and revert with a follow up to clients' queries or requests.

Get to know your colleagues. Establish a good buddy system or network system. You might call upon those colleagues to assist you in some translation projects. Also, I recommend you consider building a Translator/Editor team. This involves picking one or two of your colleagues who specialize in your field(s) of expertise, whom you have a good working relationship with and who you feel is very competent as a translator and/or editor. And forming a team with that person where you both can agree to take on projects together. You might be contacted by a company that has a very large project and they might ask you if you know other qualified translators/editors you can refer to work with you on this project; this is really a good way for you to work with a team of professionals that you feel comfortable with. It is also a great networking tool that can open doors to new clients, since that translator or editor on your team might also refer projects or new clients your way.When I look for a translator, once I'm comfortable with his or her resume and qualifications, and after having spoken to him or her, I am definitely more inclined to use the Editor/Proofreader that he/she recommends. That saves me the time to go and search for one. Of course, I always request the editor's resume as well.

Put a **Quality Control** System in place. If you work solo as a translator, without having an editor as part of your team, and you've been assigned a translation project, you already know how long you have to work on that project. Do your best to allot as much time as possible (preferably 1 or more days) to thoroughly review, edit and proofread the translation, prior to submitting it to your client. My experience has shown me that when I return to a translation a day after, once my mind has taken a break from working on it all day long, I am often in a better mind frame to detect any errors, such as **mistranslation, omission**, or simply grammatical and/or typographical errors. Even if your client informs you that your translation will be edited by an editor, it is still your full responsibility to submit an accurate and high quality translation. This is how you build your reputation as a professional translator. Another suggestion, if you are working on a large project that consumes most of your time, it might be a good idea to have a soft background music that will help you maintain the pace and relax you a bit. Also, avoid sitting in front of the computer for long hours. Make it a point to take 10 to 15 minute stretch breaks. Make sure you have a comfortable chair and even a foot and back rests. Believe me, they help tremendously!

Start building a glossary of terms for different subject matter. Build compilation of terms that you gather from work you do for your clients. This will help tremendously, i.e. Social Sciences Glossary, Legal Glossary, Medical Glossary. Because regardless of the client, you will often come across the same terms when you cover the same subject matter. This will not only save you time, but it will allow you to be consistent in your translation.

Be patient. At first it will be challenging to enter the market, because there are so many professionals already there. However, it is not impossible for you to enter. You have to be persistent, determined and resourceful.

Stay away from critical and negative people. They will drain your energy and crush your spirits. You need to be sure that your spouse or partner is supportive. Or at least, make sure you surround yourself with positive and encouraging people. There will be times when things will be very challenging and you will definitely need a shoulder to lean on, a few words of encouragement to get you going. This will all contribute to your journey, to your success.

Chapter 3
Marketing Your
Services As A Freelancer

Will you market to translation agencies only or to direct clients as well?

One of the best ways to market your services as a freelancer is by joining professional memberships. The American Translators Association or ATA is a very good one to consider. Joining the National Association of Judiciary Interpreters and Translators (NAJIT) is also another professional association to consider being a member of. Word of mouth is another way of marketing your services. Please, refer to the section on Professional Translation and Interpretation Organizations in Chapter 6 for a list of organizations.

Always acquire new skills or brush up on those you currently have to continue to be competitive. Broaden your horizon; take courses; attend seminars; read books; join online forums; attend conferences; do your own online research, for example, learn new software, know what latest versions are out there.

Join networking groups. Make sure you are listed in online directories, such as your local professional association or your national association. You need to be proactive in marketing your services. In other words, don't be shy in letting people know what you do for a living. Hand them your business cards. Set up a time to fax or email your resume with a cover letter to multiple translation companies. You can do a Google search, a Yahoo search, an online yellow page search or use other search engines to find a list of Translation Companies. You can also obtain a list from the business section of the phone book. The good thing with the Internet and with our profession, is that we do not have to limit ourselves to providing our services to local clients only. You should have no problems marketing your services to companies throughout the United States and even abroad.

ONLINE NETWORKING VENUES

The Internet allows us the opportunity to have unlimited online access to a number of networking venues that are pertinent to our profession. These venues are great ways for us to gain more exposure and to also acquire additional knowledge and find the support we need from our colleagues. I am listing here a few of those venues which will surely prove to be of great benefits to you. As you start to build your network of professional linguists and as you progress in the field and start doing your own research, you will discover many more useful sites.

Proz.com

ProZ.com, pronounced as "prose-dot-com", is an online network comprised of a group of language professionals that includes translators, interpreters, translation companies, and their clients. ProZ.com is both a marketplace and workplace where thousands of language professionals exchange job and terminology information on a daily basis.

As a language professional, you can register free of charge and this free registration will allow you to post your profile and/or resume, post queries regarding translation terms, participate in forums, and participate in other limited activities. However, a full paid membership offers an array of benefits among which you will have as a paid member: unlimited access to the Blue Board (a complete searchable database of records containing translation companies' ratings entered by translators and interpreters); front-page exposure on proz.com; automatic referrals; ability to track visits to your profile; featured or exclusive access to translation clients via the directory, job postings and Blue Board; Paid members are four times more likely than non-member site users to meet new clients.

Please go to www.proz.com for detailed information about this site.

Translatorscafe.com

Translatorscafe.com is a site that aims at providing linguists with the opportunity to search a substantial database of translation agencies, using a convenient and user-friendly application. The database was created in April-May 2002, and TranslatorsCafe.com was launched on August 1, 2002. It now has 71791 registered linguists, 4043 translation agencies and receives a stable flow of jobs.

To access the full capabilities of TranslatorsCafe.com you must be a registered user. Registration is free. After registration, you will have free access to basic features of TranslatorsCafe.com. Master members will have full access to all features of the site.

As a language professional, you can create and save your resume and cover letter, track your personal job searches and access all the information about agencies in the database.

As a registered member of TranslatorsCafe.com, you will benefit from the following: email addresses in job postings, rating of translation agencies and service providers will be displayed only to registered users; your own customized profile to highlight your uniqueness as a service provider. Your own, Web site in the form http://YourUserName.TranslatorsCafe.com. Global exposure to potential clients. Inclusion into Linguist Search results. Ability to send your bids to outsourcers who posted jobs on the Job Board. Ability to post jobs on the Job Board, participate in discussions and ask questions in the TCTerms forum. Recommendations on improving your profile. Customer service by e-mail. Automatic notifications about jobs posted on the TC Job Board. Provide your feedback on agencies and service providers whose services you used and get feedback from persons or agencies that used your services.

Please visit www.translatorscafe.com for more information.

TranslatorsBase.com

Translatorsbase.com is the leading provider of translation services via a network of global high quality service providers. Translatorsbase.com is a source of translation jobs and provides tools and services to help you bring your translation business to the next level. The online applications enable translators to reach clients from all over the world.

There are three types of users at Translatorsbase.com: 1) The Client who seeks translation services. All tools provided to clients are free of charge. Clients may search the registry, send emails to translators and agencies, save translators and agencies in the address book, post projects and ask for free translation of terms or phrases. 2) Freelance Translator who may register free of charge. They may receive messages from potential clients, list their resume in the registry, respond to posted projects and jobs, post messages on the forums, ask for free translation of terms or phrases and provide free translation of phrases to increase their search result ranking. Translators must purchase full membership in order to be able to contact potential clients, project posters and companies offering full time or part time employment. 3) Translation Agency who may register free of charge. Agencies may receive messages from potential clients, list their resume in the registry, respond to posted projects, post job offers, ask for free translation of terms or phrases and translate phrases to increase their search result ranking. Agencies must purchase full membership in order to be able to contact potential clients and project posters.

Translators and agencies must purchase full membership in order to be able to respond to inquiries from potential clients. Translators and agencies' contact information will not be displayed on their resume until they purchase full membership. Also, translators and agencies will not be able to contact individuals and companies posting translation projects. Translators will not be able to contact companies and agencies without purchasing full membership.

Translatorsbase.com also offers a wide array of services. Please visit their website at www.translatorsbase.com, for more information.

YOUR RESUME

It's very important to specify your native language on your resume. Translators translate *into* their native language. There are exceptions. They can also translate into their near-native language.

If you have a degree and/or certification in translation, make sure you specify where it was obtained. Mention any professional affiliations related to Translation/Interpretation. Always update your resume to reflect new qualifications, additional memberships, new address, new phone number, new email. Indicate any experience you might have in your field of expertise; for example, if your field of expertise is in the legal field, and you've worked as a paralegal, make sure you mention that. Mention your hobbies if they are linked to translation/interpretation. For example, if you like to fix cars or you love to read about the latest technological trends, it's worth mentioning if you translate in the field of mechanics or technology. Be sure you also include the software and hardware you use, along with their versions and specifications.

I also recommend that you create a separate email account for translation work. Try coming up with a professional email address. For example, if I see on a resume, an email address that reads: "bigdaddy@yahoo.com" and on another resume I see one that reads: "CFtranslations@yahoo.com", I guarantee, I will choose the latter. It shows me you value your professional image.

Your professional resume is your main tool that allows a potential client or hiring company to make an assessment as to who you are, what your qualifications are and what your self-image is, without even seeing you in person. It is one of the major keys that will somewhat open the doors of opportunity to you. That said, in preparing your resume, you must keep this in mind. Your resume is one of your most important marketing tools.

Make your resume professional and easy to read. Do not clutter it with unnecessary, irrelevant information not related to translation and/or interpretation. Have an objective sentence. Who are you targeting? Will you offer translation, editing, proofreading? Will you simply offer translation or editing and proofreading? If so, be sure you mention this on your resume. Will you also offer **Desktop Publishing**? The latter is not a requirement for translators; however, some translators, in order to offer a diversified service, offer desktop publishing in addition to translation. They either offer it themselves, if they have the expertise, or they work in partnership with a colleague who specializes in desktop publishing. If you do, indicate which Desktop Publishing software you use.

Write down relevant experience, mention technical skills and software you are familiar with. If you know your estimated **daily output**, mention it on your resume, include your field of expertise. Have someone else who is a native English speaker (if your resume is in English), or a native speaker of the language in which your resume is written, to proofread it before writing the final version. If you plan on marketing your services to countries outside of the United States, it is a very good idea to not only have your resume in English, but also in the other language(s) you plan to offer your translation services in.

See sample resume in Appendix C.

BUSINESS CARDS

You must have business cards printed. To start out, you can actually print your own business cards. Go to your local Office Supply store and buy the blank cards and print them using your Word Processing software. If you are not comfortable with that idea, you can do a Google or yahoo search on Business Cards, to see which online company might be able to print them for you at a reasonable rate. Be careful, make sure the cards look professional. Request a sample card from them prior to ordering your stock. You can also check the copy and print department of your local Office Supply store to see if they have great deals on business cards. If you have access to Staples or Office Max, you might want to check them out. There's also Vista Print, an online store. Their website is www.vistaprint.com.

On your business cards, you want to have your full name printed, your language pairs, you must mention whether you are a Translator and/or Interpreter, mention if you are a certified translator or registered interpreter, include your contact information, your professional e-mail address. (Refer to Resume section above to see what I mean by professional e-mail address). See Appendix D for sample business cards. Avoid selecting a card that is too flashy. Remember, you are not advertising art work. Keep it as professional and as simple as possible.

RATES

Our translation profession is under appreciated. People in general assume it is very easy to do the work we do. And because of that assumption, they tend to put a much lower price tag on our services. Well, it is up to us to first of all appreciate our profession and work for what it is. And it is our obligation, as professionals, to educate those who lack the knowledge or understanding of what our work entails.

Always make sure you review the content of the document to be translated and charge accordingly; take into account the level of technicality, how long it will take you to do the translation, when you have to return it to the client, and if you will need to do some research. Specify if you charge on **target word** (language that you are translating into) or **source word** (language that you are translating from). Keep in mind when charging on target, that some languages either contract or expand.

Be careful: there are some clients who might try to take advantage of you. For example, they might have a large document that needs translation (let's say over 4,000 words, assuming your estimated daily output is 2000 words) and request that you deliver the translation the next day. This type of request is considered as a rush request. Make sure you let them know that it will cost them more and discuss the rate upfront before accepting the assignment. If you decide to make an exception and not charge the rush, you have to let the client know beforehand, so that next time he will know you might apply the rush rate to their next rush request.

If you are not sure how much to charge, talk to your colleagues. Do some research. Contact translation companies and professional translators, request a translation estimate. Keep in mind that rates vary depending on language pairs, content, delivery deadline, document volume, document format (lots of graphs and complicated tables, for example) and text legibility. Usually a badly handwritten document will cost more than a neatly typed or neatly handwritten one.

Set competitive and realistic rates. Establish a minimum rate. If you plan to apply a rush service rate, you must first determine what you consider to be a rush service. Is a rush service a 24-hour or 48-hour delivery? Is it a delivery within 3 business days? You decide. Once you've decided, you should then establish your rush rate. It can be expressed as a percentage rate, as a flat rate or in cent per word or rate per hour. For example, I charge an additional 25% to the total translation and/or editing rate for all work delivered on a rush basis.

If you are opened to negotiation, make sure you mention it in your rate card or rate sheet. This makes a big difference in the decision-making process of the clients when they consider who they will use as translators.

If you offer volume discount, make sure it's on your rate card. If your rates do not conform with ongoing market rates (whether it's way too low or way too high), that raises a red flag, and a potential client might decide to move on to the next resume.

In your rate card, make sure you specify that your regular rate includes delivery within X number of days (business days or full days). Will you deliver within 7 business days (excluding Saturdays & Sundays) or 7 full days? This needs to be clear. Because some clients work on weekends and might consider a Saturday as a regular work day. Will you work weekends yourself? If not, will you charge extra should you decide to work on weekends and on holidays? This also needs to be specified.

TM Rates

Earlier I talked about Translation Memory software. Remember how I said that TM allows us to spend less time on translation and it also automatically provides the translation for a source segment that was already translated and stored in its database. Well, with that in mind, let's assume you receive a 10,000 word document for translation. And out of those 10,000 there are 3,000 segments (words, sentences, paragraphs, etc) that are an exact match after having ran the analysis through an existing TM. Guess what? The client who is requesting you use the TM and who has budgeted keeping these repetitious texts in mind, will also have to consider them when paying you, the translator. In other words, the client will not apply your full per source word rate on the entire 10,000 word project. He will pay you full rate for 7,000 of those words and apply an adjusted rate for the 3,000 matched words.

Trados' rates are usually broken down into the following categories based on the word analysis results: full rate on no matches (new text to be translated), adjusted rate on 100% Matches (exact match), adjusted rate on Fuzzy Matches (approximate matches), adjusted rate on repetitions (source text that is repeated). You would need to establish your Trados rates beforehand and also discuss those rates with each of your clients until you two come to an agreement. Each client applies a different Trados rate. There are some clients, however, who are willing to pay the Trados rates you have established, provided it's within their budget. I highly recommend you do your research and you have a full understanding on how these match categories work in Trados, so that you can establish reasonable rates for yourself.

At the beginning of this section, I mentioned that it is our responsibility to educate those who lack the knowledge or understanding of what our work entails. And as such, we should be sure not to allow clients to undermine the quality and value of our work. In other words, we have to be careful not to let them put a much lower price tag on our translation. On the other hand, I have to also say that one of the key factors in determining whether or not a translator's services will be solicited, is the rate charged by this translator. As a conscientious and responsible translation company owner, who values quality and whose goal is to make a profit, qualifications and rates go hand in hand, when I select my professional translators. I am usually willing to pay the few extra cents if I know I will get high quality work that is unsurpassed. However, if two translators have comparable qualifications and experience, yet there is a reasonable difference in their rates, I most certainly will select the one with the most favorable rate.

To conclude, rates are important factors which influence clients' decisions in selecting their translators. This is why, as a professional translator, we have to know or learn how to avoid undermining the value of our work, while at the same time, we must be competitive and use good judgment when providing our rates to potential clients for projects. Sometimes, it's not so bad to be a bit flexible, if we know we will get some great value in return, such as repeated work, or some large project.

YOUR CLIENTS AND YOUR WORK

Some translation companies test and grade their candidates prior to determining if the candidate should be added to their existing translators' database. For the most part, you do not get remunerated for these evaluation tests. Don't be afraid to take these tests (sample translations). Just beware, some companies take advantage of that. They sometimes send a long document of over 300 words and request a potential candidate to take it as a sample test. And guess what? This sample evaluation is an actual translation assignment. They are trying to get a freebie. A sample test should not be more than 250 to 300 words. What I've done in the past, when I've received a sample test of over 1 page to be translated, I've simply selected some parts of that text for translation and sent it to the client. All they need to do is to review and evaluate your competence in translation.

One very important point to keep in mind about your clients, is to make certain you diversify your client portfolio. In other words, try to avoid relying only on 1 or 2 clients as your major source of income. Make sure you work with a good number of clients. It's a good sign when you have a client who frequently sends you work; however it has a major disadvantage if one day, for whatever the reason, this client no longer sends you work, you're in trouble. And it might then take you a while before you build another good relationship with a new client.

When taking on an assignment with a first-time client, if you are uncomfortable with this particular client, either you feel the client is making unreasonable demands, the client is not respectful, appears to be petty, or for whatever other reason, you do not hit it off with that potential client, follow your instincts. If you still want to take a chance with the client, don't forget to do some research on the client so that you know their work ethics, find out about their payment methods (refer to the Section on Payment Issues and Collection Agencies, at the end of this Chapter for information on researching translation companies' payment methods), and get feedback from other professional translators who've worked with them. If you are not able to obtain information based on research, don't hesitate to ask the client for references. And contact those references prior to taking on the assignment.

Always ask your clients for clarification if there's something you are unsure of about the document to be translated or about their request. We often tend to assume when a client provides us with a text for translation, that this text or document is flawless. That is not often the case. When in doubt, ASK. You will be surprised to find out that sometimes the client comes back and tells you that there was an error in the text or document and that they're glad you pointed it out. Never assume, when translating. That's not our job and responsibility. When you read a text and you notice there is an error (either an incomplete sentence or thought, an omission, or any other errors), even if common sense or logic leads you to realize what is implied, do not convey this implication in your translation. Ask the client for clarification; or translate exactly as the source has it and insert a comment in the document to explain to the client that the translation is either unclear or conveys the incomplete thought or sentence because it conforms to the source text. And when delivering the project to the project manager or client, make sure you let them know to pay attention to the comment you've inserted.

Always let your client know how you will submit the work. What format you will use to deliver the project. Will it be in Word, PowerPoint, Excel, PDF format, etc.? At times, clients submit a document in PDF format and assume the translator will deliver in the same format; and they sometimes assume your translation charge includes desktop publishing. Be sure you educate your client in that sense.

Before accepting work, make sure you review the document thoroughly. Is it legible? How technical is it? Is the deadline reasonable? Do you have the necessary reference materials to accept this assignment? Is the document in just one language? Are you comfortable with the subject matter? I've come across documents written in 2 foreign languages. On some occasions, those were 2 of the languages that I work with. Since my rates vary per language pair, I made sure I charged accordingly for each language. You should also keep that in mind. And discuss these situations with your client upfront.

Never start working on a translation without written confirmation, preferably a **Purchase Order**, commonly known as **PO** from the client (See Appendix A for a Sample PO). If you've developed a long term relationship with a client and he or she verbally tells you to proceed with a project, that's another story. But as a general rule, do not proceed without a PO. You will be surprised to find out that a potential client might give you a verbal okay on a job to learn a few hours later that the job was re-assigned or cancelled by their client. If that's the case and you had already started, you're out of luck. You have no recourse. It's just your word against theirs. There are times when you will receive a Request for Urgent Quote from a client or a potential client along with a request for delivery on a specific date. Please do not take this request as a confirmation to work on the assignment. Often times, as translation companies, we receive a request for quote from one of our clients or even from a potential client and they tell us for example: "Can you work on this file and deliver by tomorrow?". We, in turn, contact our vendor and request the same. And by the time we receive our vendor's (translator's) confirmation and get back to the client, the latter either does not reply at all or waits until the end of the day to advise that they no longer need the translation. Again, that is why I am emphasizing the need to have either written e-mail authorization to proceed with the translation or a PO before proceeding with a job.

Stand by your work. Before submitting your translation to the client, always, always do a last editing and proofreading. Does your translated document reflect the same format, same layout as the source document? In other words, have you bolded, italicized, underlined, indented, the target text to reflect the same format as the source text? Is the layout of the target document identical or close to being identical to the source document, to allow the reader, whether a speaker or a non-speaker of the target language, to be able to follow the target document while referring to the source document? Did you omit any words or sentences? Does the document have any mistranslation? Have you applied the punctuation and grammatical rules of the target language? Is there consistency throughout the translation? How about the style? Does it reflect the source text, while being culturally adaptable? As translators, we must always know ahead of time who the intended **target audience** of our translated document will be. For example, if the client says that the translation should be done for an audience with a 6th grader's reading level, then, we have to be sure this is what's reflected in our translation. Avoid using "fancy" or "highly technical" vocabulary. Try to use simple vocabulary while avoiding to deviate from the actual message being conveyed in the source text. As you are translating, think about a 6th grader reading the translated text. Will he or she easily understand the text? If the source text is technical and is meant for a professional audience, then we must reflect this in our translation also.

You will encounter situations where a client will return your work edited in-house or by a third party. When reviewing, you will need to reject or accept those changes. For all instances where you've rejected the proposed correction, provide references and supporting argument to justify your translation. At times the "editor" either is not well versed in the source or target language or is not familiar with either culture or even with the actual subject. And because he or she is bilingual, he believes to be an authority in translation. The latter is not a valid justification for someone to sabotage your professional work.

In addition to working with translation companies, corporations and other types of organizations, you may also receive requests from individuals needing to have a document translated for immigration purposes, school purposes or other purposes. When the translation is to be used for immigration purposes or other types of official use, the translation must be certified and notarized.

If you choose to accept such translation assignment, you will have to provide a typed certification at the end of the translated document; this is to attest that you are qualified and/or have translation certification and that you are competent to translate the documents in the language pair requested. Then, take the document to a notary to have him or her notarize it for authentication of your signature. I highly recommend you keep a copy of the notarized document for your records prior to delivering to the client.

There are instances where a potential client might come to you with a document accompanied by its translated version, done by someone else. And this potential client may request for you to simply certify the translated document. Be very careful when you receive these requests. I personally never accept to certify someone else's translation. I simply tell the person that I only certify my own translations. If he or she so desires, I will be more than happy to provide the **certified translation** at such and such cost. Usually, this is a way for this client to avoid having to pay for your translation services. Beware that by certifying someone else's work, you are putting your professional reputation and work ethics on the line. You are also making yourself legally responsible for any error(s) in the translation. Certain States require the translation to be done by a State-approved translator.

Always strive to retain your existing clients. Build long-term relationships with them; this will result in them referring you to their colleagues.

Appreciate all your clients. Treat all jobs the same. Whether it's a 200 word project versus a 200,000 word project. Remember, your goal is to provide quality translation, and the work volume should have no impact on this commitment.

PAYMENTS

Methods

There are various ways to receive payments from translation companies and/or other clients. The most common method in the United States is via Company checks. You can also receive payments by wire transfer, Western Union, Money Gram, Money Order, Official Bank Checks, and Personal Checks. I, personally, do not accept personal checks because it is much harder to recover funds from them; remember, by the time you find out there are problems with the checks, the translation has already been delivered to the client, and it might be very difficult to get a hold of that client. Whereas, if it's a company check, for example, you have a much better chance of getting in touch with someone from the Company. However, please keep in mind that this is a matter of individual preference.

You can also receive payment via *PayPal*. PayPal is an easy way to send and receive online payments. The service allows anyone to pay in any way they prefer, including through credit cards, bank accounts, buyer credit or account balances, without sharing financial information. This is a secure way to send and request money worldwide.

PayPal has quickly become a global leader in online payment solutions with more than 164 million accounts worldwide. Available in 190 markets and 17 currencies around the world, PayPal enables global e-commerce by making payments possible across different locations, currencies, and languages.

Located in San Jose, California, PayPal was founded in 1998 and was acquired by eBay in 2002.

It's free to sign up for a PayPal account or to send money. To find out more about this service and to inquire about fees for certain services, please visit their website at www.paypal.com.

Another online payment method is via *Moneybookers*. Moneybookers enables any business or consumer with an email address to securely and cost-effectively send and receive payments online – in real-time!

With Moneybookers you can:

Send money via email from your credit/debit card or bank account; make online purchases; collect money via email.

Moneybookers delivers a product ideally suited for small businesses, online merchants, individuals and others currently underserved by traditional payment mechanisms. Moneybookers is a leading international online payment system and electronic money issuer authorised under UK and EU law and regulated by the Financial Services Authority (FSA) in the UK.

Registration with Moneybookers is free. It accepts transactions in 29 currencies.

For additional information about this service, please visit their website at www.moneybookers.com.

Another international money transfer service that is widely used is *Xoom. com*. Xoom allows you to send money in 37 countries. All transfers are made in U.S. dollars and paid either in U.S. dollars or local currency, depending on the country. For more information about Xoom, visit their website at www. xoom.com.

In addition to the payment methods mentioned above, there are other ways you might receive payment from a customer. You should address this issue with your client prior to accepting the work.

Accepting Foreign Currency Payments

If you plan to work with international clients, will you request payments in your local currency? Or will you accept foreign currency payment? If the latter applies, how will you handle that? Keep in mind if you will convert the currency into your local currency, you will have to pay exchange rate fees and sometimes additional fees depending on where you go for the transaction. Will you take that into account when charging your client for the work? Also, wire transfer payments, in general, come with additional fees. Your clients will not be responsible for those fees, unless this has been agreed upon upfront. Make sure you find out with your financial institution, what fees you will be paying for incoming wire transfers, so you can work this around your project cost. And be sure you discuss methods of payment and fees with your client before accepting to work on any projects.

With regard to international company checks, find out with your local bank or financial institution what the procedures are for depositing international checks. Find out what the hold time or clearing time is. Are there fees involved? You might want to consider the amount of money you expect to receive for that particular job, and weigh that against any fees your bank might charge, to determine if it's worth it to even accept this method of payment or even to accept the job altogether.

Invoicing

Make it a habit to send your invoices as you send your job. Most clients will not chase you down to obtain your invoice. It's your responsibility. Remember, a payment method of net 30 means you will receive payments within 30 days of the submission of your invoice. Therefore, if you wait 1 month to submit your invoice, you will receive payment within 60 days of submission of the actual project. That's not fun!

A good accounting software is very handy in keeping up with your finances, tracking your payments' due date and your financial status at a particular point in time. (Refer to Chapter 6 for a partial list of Accounting Software programs). When budgeting and in dealing with your expenses, I highly recommend you make provisions for one or two months ahead, just to account for late payments, non-payments, and job seasonality (very high season vs very low season); you need to be sure that your monthly expenses are covered. Generally, translation companies and most corporate clients pay on a net 30 and even net 45 basis. Remember, your bills won't wait!

PAYMENT ISSUES AND COLLECTION AGENCIES

What happens if you're having payment issues with one of your clients? For example, your client is over 45 days passed due and their payment method is net 30? What do you do if you've sent numerous emails as an attempt to collect payments and those emails remain unanswered? What happens if you called their Payables department many times and you have still not gotten any replies? Well, first and foremost, I recommend you document every single one of those attempts, preferably, by writing on the printed outstanding invoice, the dates, times, email addresses, phone numbers, and names of the person you emailed and/or called. Then, I suggest you write a formal letter with full details about the outstanding invoice, work or job #, date delivered, project manager's name, and attach a copy of the invoice to that letter and mail it to a specific person in the Payables Department, with a copy to the Project Manager. It's best you send this correspondence via certified mail with return receipt. That way, you have a record of when it was delivered and who signed for it. You must keep copies of the correspondence and attachment for your file. If there still is no reply or no payment, contact a collection company. Hopefully, the amount of the outstanding payment will be reasonable enough to justify this extra work and the possible fee that might be associated with soliciting the assistance of a professional collection company. If the outstanding invoice is for a minimal amount, you might want to decide to write it off as a loss after months of being outstanding.

Here is a partial list of collection companies you might want to contact:

R.M.S.

As the original collections division of Dun and Bradstreet (D&B), RMS can proudly trace its history back to 1841. In 2001, a senior management team led by David Huebner (the current Chief Executive Officer of RMS) purchased the business from D&B and established RMS as an independent business entity. RMS is now a company focused 100% on Business Process Outsourcing (BPO) and Recovery Services.

R.M.S. has U.S. offices located in 13 different states and 15 cities; Offices located in Canada, Hong Kong, India and Mexico; RMS is licensed and/or bonded to do business in every city, state, province, and international location as required by law.

For more information about their debt collection service, visit their website at www.rmsna.com or you may contact them at 1-866-329-3691.

Payment Practices

One useful site to visit prior to extending your services to a new client, is: Payment Practices.

The Payment Practices is an online database on translation and interpreting agencies and their payment behavior. The Payment Practices list was started by Karin Adamczyk, a French-English freelance translator, on December 21, 1999. The Payment Practices list was the first service intended to provide freelance translators and interpreters with information about the payment practices of translation agencies and other clients for the growing global community of translation service providers.

The Payment Practices database consists of two main components: translation agency information and responses and comments by freelancer translators and interpreters who have first-hand experience with the agencies. No hearsay or third-hand information is permitted in responses. All responses and comments are reviewed and edited if necessary to ensure the highest quality and avoid any legal problems such as charges of libel. The translation agency information includes the agency's name and contact data, and if this contact data has been verified. Translation agencies for which responses have been received are assigned scores indicating their adherence to agreed payment terms and the freelancer translator's willingness to work for that agency again.

There may also be separate comments containing pertinent information but which is not related to payment issues.

Responses are provided by freelancer translators and interpreters who have worked directly for the translation agency. Each response contains information about the agreed payment terms, when the work was performed, the amount involved, and, most important, the timeliness of payment. The freelancers also indicate if they would work for the agency again and may provide additional comments to either explain a particular situation or give additional information about their experience with that agency.

Comments are used to provide pertinent information about an agency that is not related to direct experience with payment issues. Such information may include the agency's pricing structure, project organization (or lack thereof), bankruptcy proceedings, reorganization or mergers with other agencies, or other information that may be useful to you in determining whether you wish to work for that agency.

Additionally, "alerts" are sometimes sent via email to all active members about breaking, time-sensitive news such as the filing of bankruptcy proceedings or when an individual or agency is banned from one of the translation portals. Thankfully, these alerts are rare but they do alert active members to potential losses and fraudsters.

The subscription fee for access to the Payment Practices database is just $19.99 and may be paid in a variety of means. Your subscription is valid for one year from the date payment is received. Please note that your subscription is not refundable for any reason once it has been activated as you are paying for access to the service.

For more information about Payment Practices, Inc, please visit their website at www.paymentpractices.net.

Their physical address is:
Payment Practices, Inc.
8401 Summer View Ct
Harlingen, TX 78552-6710

Proz.com Blue Board

You can also visit the Blue Board on *Proz.com* to obtain information about translation companies and their payment methods. Proz.com Blue Board is a searchable database where proz.com users enter a rating on a scale from 1 to 5, which corresponds to their likelihood of working with a translation company again. Those entries most often have comments about the translation company, and their payment practices. Paying members of Proz.com have unlimited access to records in the Blue Board. Non-members (non-paying users) may gain access to one record by either paying $0.50 per record or 50 browniz points. Browniz are points earned by contributing to the Proz.com community. You can earn those browniz points by providing site translations, introducing a new member, or by doing any other type of activity that adds value to the community.

For more information about the Proz.com Blue Board, go to their website at www.proz.com/blueboard.

You might want to visit www.collectionagencyresearch.com, an online resource for information on debt collection agencies.

FIT-Europe

FIT-Europe offers its members information on how to seek payments from bad payers in countries outside of Europe.

The FIT-Europe Steering Committee has started a project called the Bad Payers Project. Their goal is to compile all the useful information that the national associations have about their own country and to share it with the rest of the members of FIT-Europe so that they may be aware of the resources that are available in Europe to claim a debt in a different country.

The website is in both English and French.

For more information about this project, please visit their website at: http://www.fit-europe.org/

Go under the *Projects* category, select *Bad Payers* and then click on *Material Already Received*. There is information on debt collection procedures in Austria, Belgium, France, Germany, Israel, Italy, Poland, Spain, Switzerland and the United Kingdom.

BUDGETING AND FINANCIAL PLANNING

A good business owner must have his or her financial records in order. It is also important to know what the financial status of your company is. Even though you are making plans to hire an accountant for your business, that does not mean you're free from handling at least some part of the financial aspect of your company. Remember, in order for your CPA to prepare the reports and to even work with you on making quarterly or yearly projections, you have to provide him or her with the basic and relevant information. For starters, you start with opening a bank account. If you will be operating as a freelancer, the account will be opened under your name and social security. I highly recommend you use this account for your translation business only. Open a separate personal account for any other activity that is not related to your translation business. All your translation check payments should be deposited into that account. All funds for business expenses must be taken out of that account. For example, you have to consider expenses, such as purchase of dictionary and reference materials, internet connection and telephone expenses, stationery and any other business-related expenses. This will help you tremendously in making a more accurate assessment on the state of your business. It will also help come tax time. All your financial information for the business will be easier to track and gather.

If you need to use funds to make personal expenses, you can write a check from you business account, make it payable to yourself and deposit it into your personal account.

You should also consider making provisions for your retirement. Talk to your financial advisor or banker about what options are available to you. Consult your CPA also about making tax provisions. It's no fun at all, to find out you owe Uncle Sam so much in taxes because you had not paid initially on the money you earned during the fiscal year. Remember at the beginning of Chapter 2, I mentioned that as a freelancer you are responsible for your taxes. Your clients do not withhold any taxes prior to paying you.

As you make your budget and financial planning, it is important to set financial goals for yourself. For example, you can set those goals on a quarterly or even yearly basis. At the beginning, it's best to set them quarterly, since they will be more attainable. Let's say for example, you want to earn $60,000 gross income for the first year. Now, that gives you $5,000 gross a month.

You also want to set expense goals as well. This is very important, because you want to avoid having all your revenues be used for expenses and realize at the end of the year that you barely made a profit. At the beginning, you might be a bit off in your planning, however, know that it is not set in stone. If you make quarterly provisions and goals, that allows you the opportunity to adjust them as you go along to have them reflect your actual situation. If you realize you are not meeting those goals, you have to reassess your marketing strategies. Have you reached out to your target market? Have you sent enough resumes? Review your resume and make sure it is appropriate and effective in getting you the clients you need. Review your rates; are they competitive? Have you followed-up on your leads? If you have not done that, now is the time to do so. If you realize you have done everything you can, then perhaps you should reconsider the goal you set for yourself. Is it too high for the first year? Another important thing to consider when setting up your monthly goals is your monthly fixed expenses. How much are you spending every month on your regular or fixed bills? Make sure you take that into account when setting up your monthly or quarterly goals. It's always a good idea to have reserve funds to cover at least two to three months.

If you run your business from home, keep in mind that the space being used to conduct your business, is tax deductible; talk to your CPA for further details.

CHAPTER 4
LEGAL ASPECT

Reading and Signing Contracts

When you work with translation companies, they require you to sign a Freelance Agreement or Contractor Agreement prior to working with you. Some corporations and companies, might also ask you to sign a confidentiality contract before allowing you to work on their translation projects. In all of these cases, you must read the contract in its entirety. Pay careful attention to the fine print. Don't ever assume the verbiage is the same in all Agreements, even though it might appear to be. If you're not comfortable with the terms and conditions, do not sign. If you are unsure, ask for clarification. Most agencies will not assign any projects to you unless they have your signed agreement on file. If you do not agree with certain terms stipulated in the Contract, contact the client and advise that you intend to cross out the relevant sections you do not agree with; if they approve, make sure you put your initials next to those crossed out sections. Make a copy of your signed agreement and mail (do not fax) the original to the translation company while requesting they confirm receipt of the document. If the client refuses to accept the crossed out document, you will have to decide on whether or not you want to work for that client and jeopardize being held liable for any breach in that contract. Always keep copies of your Contractor Agreements. File them with their respective clients' files.

Remember: An Agreement is a legally binding contract.

Confidentiality Agreement

Generally, the Confidentiality Agreement is part of the Contractor Agreement. In some cases, the client will have a separate Confidentiality Agreement for you to sign. This is actually a very crucial part of your Agreement. As a professional translator, you will be entrusted with sensitive information and documents. It is imperative for you not to disclose any of that information to third parties. The client is trusting you with those sensitive documents; and you must respect and value their confidentiality. Even though you will be the one translating the document, you have to also understand that once you have submitted the translation to the client, this translated document becomes the exclusive property of your client. You have no access to it unless you obtain prior written consent from the client. It is very important for you to understand the implications and responsibility that come with signing a Confidentiality Agreement and a Contractor Agreement, for that matter. Again, if there are certain terms and stipulations in the Agreement that are unclear to you, please ask the client to explain before signing. If you would feel more comfortable consulting with a lawyer prior to signing, by all means you should do so.

Liability Insurance

As we all know, no one is perfect. And that means not even translators or language professionals are perfect. We would like to believe we are! But unfortunately, that is not so. Our profession requires precision, accuracy and clarity in rendering our translation, editing and even proofreading services. What may seem to us as a simple mistake, may actually cost the end-user of our translation millions of dollars, legal implications, and even their life. As an individual translator, we are responsible for the outcome of our work. As a translation company, we are also responsible for the outcome of our translation, even if we had other translators perform the actual task. Even with a quality control system in place and our commitment to accuracy and quality, there might be times when a document might have a mistake as a result of an oversight. And let's assume for a minute that the document is flawless, free from any type of error. It still does not guarantee that the client or end-user will fully be satisfied and will not decide to make some claims for compensation.

By law, a driver who owns an automobile, is obligated to purchase some sort of liability coverage, just in case there is an accident and someone or even the driver gets injured and their property gets damaged. As homeowners, we are also required to purchase homeowners' insurance. I can go on and on. You get the picture. Well, even in our profession, thankfully, we have the option of obtaining Liability Insurance in our field, referred to as **Errors and Omissions Insurance**. It is not mandatory. However, some direct clients, prior to contracting a large project, might require for the service provider (the translator or the translation company) to show proof of liability insurance. I know that through the ATA membership, members have access to a discounted Errors and Omissions Insurance through Hays Affinity Solutions. They also provide coverage for work performed by subcontractors. There is even coverage for numerical errors or mistranslation of weights and measures. Overall, Hays Affinity Solutions provides a comprehensive coverage designed specifically for the interpreting and translation industry. For more information, please call 1-866-310-4297, if you are an ATA member or you can visit them via their direct link at http://ata.haysaffinity.com.

If you are not an ATA member and would like to obtain coverage, you might want to browse the yellow pages or do an online search for Insurance Companies that provide Errors and Omissions Liability Insurance.

Bankruptcy Laws

Since this section deals with the legal aspect of our business, I would not do it justice if I did not mention this dreaded word "bankruptcy". Imagine you've worked on a very large project that took you months to complete and that you enjoyed working on mainly because you've been contemplating on the big remuneration that you will receive once the project is completed. Indeed, your project is completed and you send your very attractive invoice to your client for payment. A few months pass by and you see no sign of payment. You send numerous emails and letters, and still no sign. And months later, to your dismay you discover this client of yours has filed for bankruptcy. What recourses do you have? Who do you turn to? Can you afford to hire a lawyer?

Well, I certainly hope you will not have to face this situation. Yet, since you cannot anticipate what might happen, it does not hurt for you to stay informed and to familiarize yourself with the bankruptcy laws. If you do not know them already, learn about the different types of bankruptcies that exist and how each type might directly affect you as a vendor of that bankcrupt client. One thing for sure is that if you find yourself in this unpleasant situation, you have to hire a lawyer.

For more information about bankruptcy laws, you may visit the following website: www.uscourts.gov/bankruptcycourts/bankruptcybasics.html.

If you ever need to recover payment(s) from a client who has filed for bankruptcy, you can also contact RMS. RMS is a leading global supplier of Business Process Outsourcing and Recovery Services, with their headquarters in Bethlehem, Pennsylvania and with operations throughout the United States, Canada, Mexico, India and Hong Kong . This agency offers bankruptcy services for creditors. You can visit their website at: www.rmsna.com or call them at (866) 329-3691.

WORKING AS AN IN-HOUSE TRANSLATOR

To most translators, working as a freelance translator might seem much more appealing than working as an in-house translator. There are great advantages of working as a freelancer. For one, you work from the comfort of your home or from any location you choose to, for that matter. You can decide to even work, while you are travelling and vacationing. All you need is a computer with Internet access and your reference materials. Another good thing about being a freelancer is the fact that you do not have to deal with the daily commute. You are basically your own boss. You decide what days you want to work, what assignments you wish to accept and what hours you wish to work. If you are a night person, you may choose to do other activities during the day and save the evenings to work on your translations. Well, as they say, every situation offers its pros and cons. In this case, being a freelance translator requires that you wear many hats at once. You have to not only work on the translations, but you are responsible for running your business, managing your projects and your clients. You must also continuously work on soliciting new clients and competing with other freelancers for the same project(s). You definitely have to budget accordingly to account for seasonality that comes with this line of work.

On the other hand, working as an in-house translator (not a contractor), will not allow you the luxury listed above that you would enjoy as a freelancer; however, it guarantees that you receive a fixed salary. Most in-house translator positions also offer fringe benefits. The responsibility of managing projects and clients, for the most part lies with the project manager. One of the great advantages of working as an in-house translator is the fact that you know for sure you will receive payments regularly. Even though, most companies hardly use in-house translators nowadays, as most of their work is outsourced, you will still find some companies who are looking for in-house translators. You will find in-house translator positions in major international organizations, within the U.S. government and in some translation companies. Those companies usually have very high work volume in specific language pairs and find it more profitable to hire in-house translators as opposed to outsourcing the work. One option you certainly have should you decide to work as an in-house translator, is to still work as a freelancer in your spare time. Even though most in-house translator positions do not offer attractive salaries, most translators like the fact that they are able to receive the fringe benefits and they also have a fixed salary.

WORKING WITH AN INTERNATIONAL ORGANIZATION

Besides working with a translation company, you might prefer to work for a major international organization. There are numerous international organizations that require the expertise of in-house language professionals. Among some of the major ones, we can consider the following: The International Monetary Fund (IMF), The United Nations (UN), the World Bank, World Health Organization (WHO), and the North Atlantic Treaty Organization (NATO). Below is a brief description on each of these organizations along with their contact information. Please keep in mind that this is simply a quick reference list. You are encouraged to do your own research to obtain information about the many more international organizations that hire professional translators and/or interpreters.

THE INTERNATIONAL MONETARY FUND (IMF)

The IMF is an international organization of 185 member countries. It was established to promote international monetary cooperation, exchange stability, and orderly exchange arrangements; to foster economic growth and high levels of employment; and to provide temporary financial assistance to countries to help ease balance of payments adjustment.

Address:
International Monetary Fund
700 19th Street NW
Washington, D.C. 20431
Phone: (202) 623-7000
Website: www.imf.org

THE UNITED NATIONS (UN)

The United Nations was established on October 24, 1945 by 51 countries committed to preserving peace through international cooperation and collective security. Today, nearly every nation in the world belongs to the UN: membership totals 192 countries.

When States become Members of the United Nations, they agree to accept the obligations of the UN Charter, an international treaty that sets out basic principles of international relations. According to the Charter, the UN has four purposes: to maintain international peace and security; to develop friendly relations among nations; to cooperate in solving international problems and in promoting respect for human rights; and to be a centre for harmonizing the actions of nations.

Mailing Address:
UN Headquarters
First Avenue at 46th Street
New York, NY 10017
Phone: (212) 326-7000
Website: www.un.org

WORLD HEALTH ORGANIZATION (WHO)

WHO is the directing and coordinating authority for health within the United Nations system. It is responsible for providing leadership on global health matters, shaping the health research agenda, setting norms and standards, articulating evidence-based policy options, providing technical support to countries and monitoring and assessing health trends.

Address:
World Health Organization
Avenue Appia 20
CH - 1211 Geneva 27
Switzerland
Phone: +41 22 791 2111
Website: www.who.int

THE WORLD BANK

The World Bank is a vital source of financial and technical assistance to developing countries around the world. It is not a bank; however, it is made up of two unique development institutions owned by 185 member countries—the International Bank for Reconstruction and Development (IBRD) and the International Development Association (IDA).

Headquarters:
The World Bank
1818 H Street, NW
Washington, DC 20433 USA
Phone: (202) 473-1000
Website: www.worldbank.org

THE NORTH ATLANTIC TREATY ORGANIZATION (NATO)

NATO is an alliance of 26 countries from North America and Europe that are committed to fulfilling the goals of the North Atlantic Treaty signed on April

4, 1949. According to the Treaty, Nato's role is to safeguard the freedom and security of its member countries by political and military means.

NATO Headquarters
Blvd Leopold III
1110 Brussels, Belgium
Website: www.nato.int

WORKING FOR GOVERNMENT AGENCIES IN THE UNITED STATES

Working as a professional linguist for the U.S. government can be a very rewarding experience. Many of the government agencies in the U.S. have a great need for linguists. Your chances of working with the U.S. government greatly depend on your location, your willingness to relocate, and your language pair(s). Most of the popular languages sought after by the U.S. government are Spanish, French, Arabic and the Asian Languages. I must point out that generally, the remuneration offered by the government agencies is not an attractive one even though the workload might be quite reasonable. It should also be noted that most if not all government positions require the candidate to take a Foreign Language Test Battery. In addition to the Language Test, the candidate will undergo a Background investigation, if he or she passes the Language Test. Once the candidate passes the background investigation, he or she will receive a security clearance which is mandatory in order to work for the government. U.S. citizenship is another requirement. This process generally is a very long process, that can take from 6 months up to more than 1 year.

If you are interested in working for one of the U.S. agencies, I encourage you to visit their website for more information or to contact them directly and request information on how to submit an application. I am listing below, the name and contact information for a few of those agencies.

FEDERAL BUREAU OF INVESTIGATION (FBI)

J. Edgar Hoover Building
935 Pennsylvania Avenue, NW
Washington, D.C. 20535-0001
Phone: (202) 324-3000
Website: www.fbijobs.gov

CENTRAL INTELLIGENCE AGENCY (CIA)

Office of Public Affairs
Washington, D.C. 20505
Phone: (703) 482-0623
Website: www.cia.gov/careers

DEPARTMENT OF DEFENSE (DoD)

Defense Pentagon
Washington, D.C. 20301
Website: www.defenselink.mil/

NATIONAL VIRTUAL TRANSLATION CENTER

This organization was established in February 2003. It serves as a clearinghouse for facilitating the use of translators among the different U.S. agencies. Candidates must be U.S. citizens.

Mailing Address:
National Virtual Translation Center
Suite NVTC-200
935 Pennsylvania Ave. N.W.
Washington, D.C. 20535
Website: www.nvtc.gov

U.S. DEPARTMENT OF STATE

U.S. Department of State
2201 C Street NW
Washington, DC 20520
Phone: (202) 647-4000
Website: www.state.gov

You can also visit www.usajobs.com for postings on available government jobs.

Chapter 5
Running Your Translation Company

As I mentioned previously, a professional translator, may decide to work on a freelance basis only or may decide to run a translation company. By choosing the latter, you are able to offer a wider selection of language pairs, besides your own. Furthermore, by running a business, you are able to get more exposure on the market.

A translation company can be made up of just one person, the translator, or can have as many as hundreds of employees, or even more. I should also note that some freelancers decide to incorporate and work under a business name to protect themselves against certain liabilities and to also address tax issues. These freelancers might choose not to extend their services beyond the scope of their language pair(s). The bottom line is, you are the only one to decide whether or not you want to incorporate; whether or not you want to limit your services to your language pair(s) only, or whether or not you would like to offer additional language pairs, and to outsource the work. In making your decision, you have to do thorough research, consider the expenses involved and weigh them against the possible returns. Do you have great discipline? Do you have the financial resources to set-up the business? Do you plan on running the business from your home or do you plan on renting outside office space? If you want to run it from home, do you have a dedicated space that will allow you to accommodate the business? If you want to run it from an outside office location, how much will that cost? Do you have enough demands for your services that will allow you to cover the cost of running the business in an outside office while being able to pay your translators and possibly your employees, if you choose to hire additional staff?

Will you be the one running the business or will you hire an office Manager? How long do you estimate it will take you to break-even and to eventually start earning a profit? These are some of the important questions you will need to ask yourself before making your decision.

Once you have made your decision and you feel comfortable with it, your next step should be to decide on the business structure. I will not go into great details here. I will simply suggest you read some books about the different types of business structures and the advantages versus disadvantages that exist between each one. You have to decide whether you want to run a sole proprietorship, a partnership, a limited liability company, an S Corp or any other type of corporation. Then, once you have an idea based on your research, you should consult with a business lawyer and an accountant. Refer to the section at the end of this Chapter "Choosing your Professional Team" for some insights on how to select a lawyer and a CPA.

Now here comes the fun part: coming up with a company name. More than likely, you have thought about it long before you've reached that point. Once you decide on a name, research it online and in business/trade journals and through other relevant sources to make sure it does not already exist. You might be surprised! Just when you thought you've come up with an original and special name, someone else might have already selected that name. After you've decided on the business structure and you've settled on an official name, you have to file a request for a **EIN** or **Employer Identification Number**, then you have to register the business with your State. Each State has its own requirements for business filing. Find out with your particular State what else is required in order to register your business. You can choose to do so by yourself or you can have a business lawyer who specializes in business formation to file and handle the entire registration process on your behalf.

Besides obtaining your business's EIN, there is also another important number you might consider applying for. It is a **DUNS** number. A DUNS number is a nine digit number issued by Dun & Bradstreet, commonly known as D&B, that allows a business to be listed on D&B's database. With a DUNS number, a company's credit information is available to other companies, to banks and to other potential creditors. D&B, is the world's leading source of commerical and business information. Visit their website for more information about them: www.dnb.com.

MARKETING YOUR SERVICES AS A COMPANY

Website

Once you have registered your translation business and all is in order, consider yourself officially ready to be in business. What you need to do now is to make your company known to the outside world. One of the first important steps to take is to consider having a website. That will allow you to have a great online presence. Depending on your budget, you may opt to create your website on your own. There are many software programs that will allow you to do that. Here is a list of some of those software programs: FrontPage (www.microsoftfrontpage.com); Adobe Dreamweaver (www.adobe.com); Web Easy Professional (www.webeasyprofessional.com); Web Studio (www.webstudio.com); Web Plus (www.serif.com); Web Page Maker (www.webpage-maker.com); and Site Spinner (www.virtualmechanics.com). Once again, you are encouraged to research the products before making your selection and in order to purchase the one that will best suit your needs and be compatible to your hardware specifications. If you are like me, rather than venturing into this "do-it-yourself" website project, you will enlist the services of a professional web developer. It's also a good idea to ask for client references when selecting your web developer.

Other ways to advertise

Another way to market your services is to have brochures printed, write newsletters, and one of the least expensive ones is to print your own flyers and to even write your marketing letters to be mailed out to potential clients. Advertising online and in print directories and in phone books should also be considered.

Of course there are a number of ways in which you can gain exposure and solicit clients. Those are just the main ones. Depending on your budget and on how aggressive you want to be in your marketing strategies, I suggest you get together with a business consultant so that you both can devise a business plan that will be the blueprint for your business.

Carline Férailleur-Dumoulin

ACCEPTING CREDIT CARD PAYMENTS

The majority of businesses accept credit cards as their methods of payment. When you accept to process credit card payments, this allows you to receive immediate compensation for your services. In general, the funds get credited to your bank account within 24 to 48 hours. For these transactions, the client does not have to be present in order for you to charge the card. Of course, you must obtain your client's authorized signature prior to charging the card. This is one sure way for you to secure payments. Yes, there are fees involved when you accept credit card payments. However, those fees might be minimal when you consider the benefits you will obtain. I should also point out that from a customer's standpoint, the fact that your company accepts credit cards, adds a certain prestige or even greater recognition to your company. For over 4 years, I have used the services of NOVA Information Systems, now operating under the name of Elavon, for my credit card processing. As an ATA member, you receive special rates when you open a merchant account with Nova. Their website is www.novainfo.com.

You may also want to look into different merchant account processing providers and compare their rates and services prior to making your final selection.

YOUR CLIENTS

If you recall in Chapter 2, as part of your auto-analysis and assessment, in helping you decide whether or not you would enter the field of translation and whether or not you would run your company, one of the key questions was: who will your target audience be?

Well, you are a freelancer who already has an audience. Now that you have decided to run your company and to offer additional languages, you need to ask yourself that same question. Who will my target audience be? Will you work with other translation companies only? Will you work with individuals? With corporations (domestic and foreign)? Will you even consider being a direct supplier to the government? Once you have answered those questions and decided on who your clientele will be, you will now be able to concentrate on getting those clients.

60

If you decide to be a direct supplier to the U.S. government, you have to go through a few channels and some lengthy processes. I will not go into great details here, because this category requires a whole chapter and even an entire book devoted to it. There are a good variety of books and publications that deal with working with the federal government. You may consult the ATA publications, your local bookstore or refer to online resources.

Here are a few good sites to refer to and browse through to allow you the opportunity to familiarize yourself with this process: www.fedbizopps. gov (Federal Business Opportunities); www.gsa.gov (U.S. General Services Administration); www.ccr.gov (Central Contractor Registration); www.dnb. com (Dun & Bradstreet); www.nasbc.org (National Association of Small Business Contractors); www.sba.gov (U.S. Small Business Administration). A good book reference is "Getting a GSA Schedule" written by Scott Orbach and Judith Nelson (ISBN: 1-4196-3264-7); their website: www.EZGSA. com.

As a new company, it might be a challenge to enter into this federal procurement process. A good way to get your foot in the door is if you either pair up with a larger company to enter the bidding process, or if you choose to be a subcontractor to the company that has won the government bid. The latter is a good way for you to gain exposure, to acquire experience with government projects and to build references when you will be ready to bid yourself. You can also choose to advertise in directories that target government entities only.

As you can see, there are many options available to a translation company in terms of offering translation and related language services to a wide array of clients and sectors. It is up to you to decide if you will contemplate one, more than one, or all of these options. Keep in mind, however, that without a good marketing approach, without doing the necessary research, without a good professional team on your side, and of course without the necessary capital, you will limit yourself and your company. Again, patience is a key virtue to adopt when starting out.

Whoever said that the road to success was an easy one!

YOUR VENDORS

In the preceding chapters, I talked about you being the vendor. Other terms often used to refer to vendors in our field are: translators, freelancers, contractors. Even though each of these terms has their own meaning, which is not exactly similar to each other, the bottom line is that all of them, the translator, the freelancer, the contractor and the vendor, they all sell their services, which is what a vendor does.

Now that you have decided to have your own company and you've decided to expand your services beyond the scope of your language pairs, you too are now in a position to work with vendors. Please note that the term vendor is a pretty broad term. For the purpose of this book, I will use the word vendor or vendors to refer to translators. However, a vendor can also be another of your suppliers that offers goods or services other than translation and/or editing.

How do you go about building your vendors' database? How do you verify the credentials, level of expertise, work ethics and reliability of your vendors? Well, that should not be a foreign concept to you, considering you are a vendor yourself and you have a pretty good idea on how a potential client screens and selects his or her vendors. First and foremost, you should gather information on the reliable and reputable referral resources where you know you will be able to find those vendors. You will of course, use the same venue that you, yourself utilized in order to advertise your professional services. In addition, use your colleagues and your other vendors as references. Refer to the Section on Marketing your services as a freelancer, found in Chapter 3 for the partial list of reliable resources.

Once you have contacted your potential vendor, reviewed his or her resume and rates, it is a good idea to request professional references. It will be up to you to know if you will also set-up a Translation Evaluation System, where you will request those vendors to take sample translation tests. This will include having reliable translators/editors on board who will be competent enough to grade and provide you with a thorough assessment of the sample translation. In that case, you will have to pay the evaluator for his or her services.

Again, this decision is up to you.

Build a Database that will allow you to enter information such as the full name, contact information, language pairs, field of expertise, and other relevant information about your vendors. This of course will be in addition to having hard copy files of the resumes and all other required documents, such as rate sheet, signed W-9, and signed Service and Confidentiality Agreement(s).

You will need to draft your own Service Agreement to have the vendors sign. I highly recommend you seek legal counsel when drafting the Service Agreement and Confidentiality Agreement. Remember, that Agreement becomes a legal contract that will bind you, your company, and the vendor. It is not to be taken lightly. It is imperative for you to do this the right way in order to protect yourself and your company legally.

As I previously mentioned, I will not elaborate any further on the legal, financial and business aspects involved in working with vendors. You will need to do more research into this process and obtain the necessary professional advice, prior to undertaking this venture.

In contemplating using the services of vendors, you will also need to consider whether or not you will use both domestic and foreign/international vendors. If you decide to work with the latter, be sure you request references from them. You should get both foreign and domestic professional references from these non-domestic vendors. You need to confirm their work ethics and feel comfortable that they will not only abide by your terms and conditions, but that they will respect your request for confidentiality.

Some foreign vendors might request payment upfront. I do not particularly like that concept. However, use your best judgement. How large is the project? How much money are we talking about? How qualified is this particular vendor to do the work at hand? How does he/she compare to a domestic vendor? Will this vendor be willing to accept 10% upfront, as opposed to the full payment? This is a tricky situation to be in! For example, I've worked with a few Canadian vendors who request payment upfront before accepting a project. I usually pay them via PayPal. Their reasoning is as follows: by the time they receive payment, the exchange rate might have fluctuated and affect them negatively. A Net 30 payment agreement means they receive the check after 30 days of submitting their invoice and have to wait at least another week for the payment to clear at their financial institution, since it is a foreign check. And in some cases, the value of the payment by the time they have access to the funds has decreased. Also they might have to pay fees if they don't have a US dollar account and need to convert the US payment into CAD dollars. Besides PayPal payments, what other methods of payment does this vendor accept?

Beware however that some foreign vendors might not be familiar with the culture in either the source or target country. It's important to select vendors that are familiar with both cultures and customs and have the necessary expertise and experience in specific fields. Do they use translation tools? Do they work with the latest software? What is the time zone difference? Will they be able to deliver the project on time? How frequently do they check their emails?

Now on to another important topic: your financial obligation towards your vendors. As we know, if you are looking to work with a vendor, it's certainly because you've received a request for translation from a client. Once you've sent the Purchase Order to your vendor, and you both have agreed on the assignment and terms of payment, you automatically have a financial obligation to that vendor. If you've agreed to pay him or her on a net 30 or net 45 basis, be sure to respect that commitment, regardless of whether or not your client has paid you. This is a good reason why you should make payment provisions for your vendors.

Words of Advice

Treat all your vendors well. They are your internal customers. Pay them promptly. Make provisions for their payments. Because even if you don't receive payments on time, or you don't receive payments at all from your clients, you still made an agreement with them that you will pay them for their job. Honor your word and you will earn their respect. They will be your best allies. Remember, without them, you have no Company. Treat them as you would like to be treated as a freelancer, or vendor. And make sure you ask your employees and project managers to treat them just the same. Build your business on Integrity!

CHOOSING YOUR PROFESSIONAL TEAM

As the owner of a translation company, you will soon realize that you no longer are the sole individual who holds the key to your company's success. The success of your company will depend on the entire team you will select to work side by side with you. This means from your clients, to your subcontractors, to your internal staff, should you choose to hire employees. What is also important is for you to have a solid team. This definitely includes your other professional team that is comprised of your Accountant (CPA), your Lawyer or Legal Advisor, your Web developer, your Banker and even your Business Consultant. There are many resources out there that will allow you to make your selection. You can search online, through the yellow pages, talk to your colleagues, family and friends for referrals. I suggest you write down a list of questions that specify what you are looking for in each of these professionals. See the following 2 pages for a suggestion on what to look for and on a list of questions you might ask during your selection process. You can also use this information as reference when looking for other professionals.

CPA INFORMATION

FIRM OR CPA NAME:

CONTACT PERSON'S NAME:

ADDRESS:

PHONE NUMBER:

EMAIL ADDRESS:

WEBSITE ADDRESS:

HOW LONG HAS THE COMPANY/CPA BEEN IN BUSINESS?

WORKING HOURS:

SERVICES OFFERED: Do they offer 1 time consultation? Do they offer Tax and Business planning? Do they offer bookkeeping services? Do they prepare financial statements, and do they offer financial statements' review? Do they prepare monthly and/or quarterly financial statements? Do they cater to small businesses? Do they provide payroll and tax returns preparation? Do they offer unlimited consultation free of charge? Do they offer pick-up and delivery services of financial records? Do they provide QuickBooks or other Accounting software training? If so, what are the fees?

RATES: Do they charge per hour? Do they charge quarterly or monthly?

REFERENCES: Need to have them provide you with at least 3 client references. Here are a few questions, you might want to consider asking the references for your assessment: Are their services timely? Are they professional? Would you consider them to be good advisors? How long have you been using their services? Have you used other CPA's services prior to them? If so, how would you compare them with the previous CPA's? What made you decide to select them as your CPA.

SCHEDULED APPOINTMENT FOR 1 ON 1 MEETING: Is there a charge for this first time meeting?

Appointment Date and Time:

BUSINESS LAWYER INFORMATION

FIRM OR LAWYER'S NAME:

CONTACT PERSON'S NAME:

ADDRESS:

PHONE NUMBER:

EMAIL ADDRESS:

HOW LONG HAS THE FIRM/LAWYER BEEN IN PRACTICE?

LENGTH OF TIME IN PRACTICE IN YOUR PARTICULAR STATE?

WORKING HOURS:

SERVICES OFFERED: Do they offer Business Formation services; contracts preparation and/or revision? Employment Contracts? Preparation of Agreements and Contracts?

RATES: Hourly rate; minimum rate?

REFERENCES: Need to have them provide you with at least 3 client references. Here are a few questions, you might want to consider asking for your assessment.

Are there services timely? Are they professional? Would you consider them to be good advisors? How long have you been using their services? Have you used other lawyers or law firms' services prior to them? If so, how would you compare them with the previous ones? What made you decide to select them as your lawyers.

SCHEDULED APPOINTMENT FOR 1 ON 1 MEETING: Is there a charge for this first time meeting?

Appointment Date and Time:

Chapter 6
Internet Scam Alert

Even in our line of work, we have to look out for scams. There are a couple of email scams going on targeting translators and interpreters. Some of those email scams involve a request for quote for translation and typesetting services for the Regulatory Affairs Professionals Society. Although the email requests are part of a scam, the Regulatory Affairs Professionals Society is a legitimate organization. What you must also look for is the sender's email address. Usually, the email addresses either come from personal email addresses or very questionable addresses. Be sure to stay alert when you receive any kind of odd requests for translation and interpretation. I've also received quite a few email scams from someone claiming to be writing on behalf of a prince or high ranking official in some part of Africa, needing interpreting services for their visit to the United States or request for interpreting services for someone who will be attending a seminar or conference in a particular State.

Here is an excerpt from an ATA Article by the ATA's Executive Director Walter W. Bacak, Jr. addressing these Internet scams:

"The authors (perpetrators) of the scams include the recipient's name, email address, and the recipient's primary non-English language embedded in the text of the message, which adds some credibility. After the recipient (ATA member) responds to the message confirming his or her availability, the author expresses a check (which is a fake or drawn on a closed account) with instructions to notify the author as soon as the check is received. A couple days later, the author emails the member canceling the assignment—the daughter or client got sick. The author then tells the member to keep $xxx for your time and trouble and wire the remainder to xxx [some other person]. BEWARE: if you wire the author the funds, you are liable for the entire amount, according to the National Consumer League. For more information on this "fake check scam," please visit the National Consumers League's Internet Fraud Watch website at http://fraud. org/tips/internet/fakecheck.htm "

If you would like to obtain more information about this issue from the ATA, please visit the following link: www.atanet.org//ata_activities/internet_ scams.php

If you believe you've been a victim of Internet Crime, you are encouraged to file an online complaint at www.ic3.gov. The Internet Crime Complaint Center (IC3) was established as a partnership between the Federal Bureau of Investigation (FBI) and the National White Collar Crime Center (NW3C) to serve as a means to receive Internet related criminal complaints and to further research, develop, and refer the criminal complaints to federal, state, local, or international law enforcement and/or regulatory agencies for any investigation they deem to be appropriate. The IC3 was intended, and continues to emphasize, serving the broader law enforcement community to include federal, as well as state, local, and international agencies, which are combating Internet crime and, in many cases, participating in Cyber Crime Task Forces.

You will also find on that site, a list of different Internet Crime Schemes and what's involved in each one. This is a very insightful sight.

PROFESSIONAL TRANSLATION & INTERPRETATION ORGANIZATIONS IN THE UNITED STATES AND ABROAD
(THIS IS NOT AN ALL INCLUSIVE LIST)

ARGENTINA

Asociación Argentina de Traductores e Intérpretes (AATI)

The Argentine Association of Translators and Interpreters (AATI) was founded in 1982 by a group of professionals. AATI's goal is to represent and protect the interests of literary and technical-scientific translators and interpreters. Promote professional improvement. Encourage collaboration and exchange of knowledge and professional experience as well as establish relationships among AATI's members and other associations, educational institutions and organizations. Contribute to spreading translation and interpretation activities.

Their website address is: www.aati.org.ar/

Asociación de Intérpretes de Conferencias de la Argentina (ADICA)

ADICA, the Argentine Association of Conference Interpreters, was founded on October 2, 1979. Its key objective is to represent simultaneous and consecutive professional interpreters in Argentina, to extend the improvement and meaning of their activities and to benefit from an association which defends its members' interests and underscores the profession's prestige.

Their website address is: www.adica.org.ar/

AUSTRALIA

Australian Institute of Interpreters and Translators (AUSIT)

The Australian Institute of Interpreters and Translators (AUSIT) is the national association for the translating and interpreting profession. It was founded in 1987, bringing together existing local associations and specialist groups and now has branches in each State and Territory. AUSIT is a member of the International Federation of Translators (FIT), where it represents the interests of members and takes part in the development of international policies likely to affect the future of the profession, and in initiatives to promote and support translation associations throughout the world.

> AUSIT National Office:
> PO Box 193 Surrey Hills VIC 3127
> Phone: + 61 3 9895 4473
> Website: www.ausit.org

National Accreditation Authority for Translators and Interpreters (NAATI)
NAATI is a national standards body owned by the Commonwealth, State and Territory Governments of Australia. It is a company limited by guarantee under the Commonwealth Corporations Law 2001. NAATI is also an advisory body for the Translation and Interpreting (T & I) industry in Australia providing advice and consultancy services on T & I standards, accreditation, role and conduct of Translators and Interpreters and T & I skills in various settings.

NAATI accreditation is the only credential officially accepted for the profession of translation and interpreting in Australia. All government Translation and Interpreting (T & I) services require translators and interpreters to be NAATI accredited whenever possible.

> NAATI National Office:
> 17A 2 King Street
> Deakin ACT 2600
> Phone: +61 2 6260 3035
> Website: www.naati.org.au/

AUSTRIA

Austrian Association of Certified Court Interpreters (AACI)
The Austrian Association of Court Interpreters is a nonpolitical, nonprofit organization existing for more than 75 years with the declared objective of furthering the professional and business interests of sworn and certified court interpreters in Austria. The Association is a member of the Fédération

Internationale des Traducteurs (FIT) and of the Austrian Association of Sworn and Certified Court Experts.

Postal Address:
A-1016 Vienna, PO box 14
Phone: +43 / 1 / 479 65 81
Website: www.gerichtsdolmetscher.at/

European Society for Translation Studies (EST)
EST, the European Society for Translation Studies, is an international society of translation and interpreting scholars. EST was founded in Vienna, Austria in September 1992. EST Membership is open to individual scholars and academic and other institutions in Europe and beyond.

Their website address is: www.est-translationstudies.org

BELGIUM

Belgian Chamber of Translators, Interpreters and Philologists/
(Chambre belge des traducteurs, interprètes et philologues / Belgische Kamer van Vertalers, Tolken en Filologen [CBTIP/BKVTF])
The Belgian Chamber of Translators, Interpreters and Philologists, is a non-profit organization, founded in 1955. In order to become a member, an individual must hold a university degree in a field of linguistic; or he/she must pass the examination administered to individuals with at least 4 years of professional experience in the field of translation, as the main profession.

Address:
Rue Montoyerstraat 24
b12 1000 Bruxelles
Phone: 02/513.09.15
Website: www.cbtip-bkvtf.org

BRAZIL

Associação Brasileira de Tradutores (ABRATES)

ABRATES, the Brazilian Association of Translators, is a professional association that brings together professionals and institutions in the field of translation, with the objective of promoting professional development, disseminating information and encouraging interchange and activities that aim at promoting the value of these professionals and this profession.

Address:
Av. Graça Aranha 145/304
Centro, Rio de Janeiro - RJ
CEP 20030-003
 Phone: (21) 2522-1083
Website: www.abrates.com.br/

Sindicato Nacional dos Tradutores (SINTRA)

SINTRA is an organization that represents translators and interpreters in all fields, and throughout Brazil. It was founded in November 30th,. 1988 in Rio de Janeiro.

Address:
Rua da Quitanda
194/Salas 1206/1207
Centro – Rio de Janeiro – RJ
CEP 20-091-000
Phone: 55 (21) 2253-1616
Website: www.sintra.org.br/

CANADA

Association of Translators and Interpreters of Alberta (ATIA)

The Association of Translators and Interpreters of Alberta / Association des traducteurs et interprètes de l'Alberta (ATIA) is the only association of certified translators and conference interpreters in the province of Alberta. The Association was founded in 1979 and is the only member for Alberta of

The Canadian translators, terminologists and Interpreters Council (CTTIC). Through CTTIC, the Association is affiliated with International Federation of Translators (FIT).

Mailing Address:
P.O. Box 546
Main Post Office
Edmonton, AB
T5J 2K8
Phone: 780.434.8384
Website: www.atia.ab.ca/

Association of Translators and Interpreters of Manitoba (ATIM)/ Association des traducteurs et interprètes du Manitoba

The Association of Translators, Terminologists and Interpreters of Manitoba (ATIM) was incorporated in 1980. It is a non-profit association and an affiliate of the Canadian Translators, Terminologists and Interpreters Council (CTTIC). The objectives of the Association are to provide a collective voice for its members, to ensure that members exercise their profession in accordance with its Code of Ethics, and to protect the public interest by ensuring the quality of the services rendered by its members.

Address:
ATIM
200 Ave. de la Cathédrale, Box 83
Winnipeg, Manitoba
R2H 0H7 Canada
Phone: (204) 797-3247
Website: www.atim.mb.ca/

Association of Translators and Interpreters of Nova Scotia (ATINS)

The Association of Translators and Interpreters of Nova Scotia ATINS) was founded with the following objectives:

To give translators and interpreters of the province the opportunity to meet and discuss matters of common concern, and to provide a link with translators and interpreters of other provinces and countries;

To promote the profession and development of its members;

To give users of translation services access to a body of competent professionals

Mailing Address:

ATINS

P.O. Box 372

Halifax, N.S.

B3J 2P8

Website: www.atins.org

Association of Translators and Interpreters of Ontario (ATIO)
Association des Traducteurs et Interprètes de L'Ontario

The Association of Translators and Interpreters of Ontario (ATIO) is the oldest organization of translators, conference interpreters, court interpreters and terminologists in Canada. It was founded in 1920 as the Association technologique de langue française d'Ottawa, and was incorporated the following year under Ontario Letters Patent. In 1962 the Association adopted its current name. ATIO is also the first translators' association in the world whose certified members are deemed professionals by law, for in February 1989 the Province of Ontario granted a reserved title for certified members of ATIO through the Association of Translators and Interpreters Act, 1989. The main purpose of the Association is to promote a high level of competence in the fields of translation, conference interpretation, court interpretation and terminology by: providing a collective voice for its members, promoting the professional development of its members, and applying standardized, national criteria to recognize the competence of professional translators, conference interpreters, court interpreters and terminologists.

Address:

1 Nicholas Street

Suite 1202

OTTAWA, ON K1N 7B7

Toll Free: 1 800-234-5030

Phone: 613.241.2846

Website: www.atio.on.ca/

Fédération Internationale des Traducteurs (FIT) / International Federation of Translators

FIT is an international federation of associations of translators, interpreters and terminologists gathering more than 100 associations from all over the world. Its purpose is to promote professionalism in the disciplines it represents. FIT is also concerned with the conditions of professional practice in various countries and strives to defend translators' rights in particular and freedom of expression in general.

Mailing Address:
International Federation of Translators
2021 Union Avenue, Suite 1108
Montréal (Québec) H3A 2S9, Canada
Phone: (514) 845-0413
Website: www.fit-ift.org

Literary Translators' Association of Canada (LTAC) / Association des Traducteurs et Traductrices Littéraires du Canada

Since its inception in 1975 the Literary Translators' Association of Canada (LTAC/ATTLC) has sought to promote literary translation and to protect the interests of its members throughout the country. For most of its existence, the Association has enjoyed the support of the Canada Council for the Arts.

Today the LTAC has approximately one hundred and twenty members. Although the majority translate works originally written in French or English, many work in other languages: Czech, Italian, German, Polish, Danish, Norwegian, Lithuanian, Russian, Dutch, Punjabi, Arabic, Yiddish and Spanish, to name a few.

Mailing Address:
Literary Translators' Association of Canada (LTAC)
LB 601 Concordia University
1455, boul. De Maisonneuve ouest
Montréal (Québec), H3G 1M8
Phone: (514) 848-2424 ext 8702
Website: www.attlc-ltac.org

Society of Translators and Interpreters of British Columbia (S.T.I.B.C.)

The Society of Translators and Interpreters of British Columbia (S.T.I.B.C.) was incorporated in 1981. It is a non-profit professional association and an affiliate of the Canadian Translators Terminologists and Interpreters Council (CTTIC). S.T.B.I.C.'s goal is to promote the interests of translators and interpreters in British Columbia and to serve the public by providing a Code of Ethics that members agree to abide by and a system of Certification for translators and interpreters.

Contact Information:
S.T.I.B.C.
Office Administrator
Suite 511, 850 West Hastings Street
Box 33
Vancouver, British Columbia (Canada) V6C 1E1
Phone: (604) 684-2940
Website: www.stibc.org

CHILE

Colegio de Traductores e Intérpretes de Chile (COTICH)

The Chilean Association of Translators and Interpreters, COTICH (formerly AGTS) is a legally established Chilean non-governmental organization and is a member of the Fédération Internationale des Traducteurs, FIT.

It was founded in 1991 to protect the interests and regulate the practice of the translating profession, promote the advancement of its members, and contribute effectively to Chile's economic, cultural and social development.

Its members are bound by a strict code of professional ethics designed to ensure optimal standards of integrity, efficiency, and confidentiality .

Address:
Luis Thayer Ojeda 95
Of. 207
Providencia – Santiago CHILE
Phone: (56 2) 251-2887
Website: www.traductores-agts.cl/

CHINA

Honk Kong Translation Society

Hong Kong Translation Society was incorporated in October 1971. It is a non-profit society, with the objective to enhance the standard and professionalism of translation (both oral and written) in Hong Kong. It became a registered charitable organization with the Hong Kong Government in 1991 on the grounds of education promotion. It has become a member association of the Translators Association of China since 1986 and of the Federation Internationale des Traducteurs (FIT) since 1988.

Address:
PO BOX 20186
Hennessy Road
Post Office
Hong Kong
Phone: (852) 27889648
Website: www.hkts.org.hk/

Translators Association of China

The Translators Association of China (TAC) was founded in 1982. As the only national association in the field of translation in China, it functions as an academic as well as professional association. Made up of institutions, enterprises, associations and individuals all over the country engaged in translation and interpretation, on a voluntary basis, TAC has group, corporate and individual members in China's 34 provinces, municipalities, autonomous regions and special administrative regions.

Address:
Wai Wen Building
24 Baiwanzhuang Street
Beijing 10037
Phone: 86 10 68995897
Website: www.tac-online.org.cn

COLOMBIA

Asociación Colombiana de Traductores e Intérpretes (ACTI)

This is a non profit Association founded on June 15, 1998 by a group of translators and interpreters of various nationalities. It seeks to promote professionalism in the fields of translation and interpreting.

Address:
Calle Bogotá
D.C. Colombia
Phone: (57-1) 648-0761
Website: www.traductorescolombia.com

ECUADOR

Asociación de Traductores e Intérpretes del Ecuador (ATIEC)

This Association was legally established on September 12, 2007. It was founded as a result of the numerous informal service offers in translation in various languages and to also provide mutual support for translators and interpreters. It is made up of professional translators and interpreters, both foreign and national. It seeks to guarantee quality translation and interpretation through a system of certification and training and through publications and workshops, organized periodically.

Address:
Calle Guerrero 1254
Bossano Edif. Montealto, Depto 9
Quito, Ecuador
Phone: 593 (0) 3 2-243-2723
Website: www.atiec.org

FINLAND

Association of Finnish Translation Companies (SKTOL)

The Association of Finnish Translation Companies serves both translation companies and users of translation services by promoting the professional expertise of member companies and by enhancing the quality of translation services.

Address:
PO Box 309
FI-00121 Helsinki
Finland
Website: www.sktol.org

FRANCE

Association des Traducteurs Littéraires de France (ATLF)

The main objective of the ATLF is to defend the specific interests of the literary translators and to promote the quality of the translations.

Address:
99 rue de Vaugirard
75006 Paris
Phone: (+33) 1 45 49 26 44
Website: www.atlf.org

Association Professionnelle des Métiers de la Traduction (APROTRAD)

APROTRAD was founded in 1993, having as objectives, to foster dialogue between colleagues who work in isolation, to instruct high-school and university students in the best ways to access the professions of translator and interpreter, to give the general public and clients a true perception of our profession, and to work towards official and legal recognition of our profession at French and European levels. It also provides training to its members.

Address:
46 ter, rue Sainte Catherine
45000 Orléans
France
Phone: (33) 2 48 65 0431
Website: www.aprotrad.org

Société Française des Traducteurs (SFT)
Société Française des Traducteurs (SFT) is a national trade association located in France, with over 1000 members (translators and interpreters). Contact Information:

Société Française des Traducteurs (SFT)
CERTEX
22, rue de la Pépinère
75008 - Paris
Website: www.sft.fr

GREECE

Panhellenic Association of Professional Translators (PAPT)
The Association aims to study, protect, promote and safeguard the financial and professional interests of the Association's members, principally in the field of translation copyright.

Address:
M. Drakou 28
GR 11476 - Athens
Phone: (+30) 1 646 0233
Website: www.psem.gr/

GUATEMALA

Asociación Guatemalteca de Intérpretes y Traductores (AGIT)
AGIT is a non-profit, apolitical and professional Association. It has been around for more than 20 years. It's comprised of a number of experienced translators and interpreters. Its main objective is to defend the legal, economic, moral and social interests of translators and interpreters in Guatemala.

Address:
6a Avenida 14-21
Zona 9, Interior Oficina I
Guatemala City, Guatemala
Phone: (502) 362-6305
Website: www.agitguatemala.org

INDIA

Indian Translators Association (ITAINDIA)

ITAINDIA is a non-profit Association that seeks to unite the widespread translators and interpreters community of India at a common platform to address issues for betterment of the industry and take steps to ensure that its members provide services meeting professional standards of the industry.

Address:
K-5/B, Lower Ground Floor,
Kalkaji, New Delhi -110019
Phone: +91(011) 26291676
Website: www.itaindia.org

ITALY

Associazione Italiana Traduttori e Interpreti (AITI)

AITI, founded in Biella, Italy in 1950, is a non-profit professional association of translators and interpreters. It is a founding member of the International Federation of Translators and a founding member of CEATL (the European Council of Associations of Literary Translators).

Address: c/o Stuido Bianchi
Viale delle Milizie 9
00192 Roma
Phone: 39 347 240 45 31
Website: www.aiti.org

Associazione Nazionale Interpreti di Conferenza Professionisti (ASSOINTERPRETI)

Founded in 1974, Assointerpreti, the Italian Association of Conference Interpreters, has a membership of practising professional simultaneous and consecutive interpreters from all over Italy. Assointerpreti is a member of Assiterm (Italian Terminology Association), CoLAP (Coordinamento Libere Associazioni Professionali), and **Italcongressi PCO Italia,** (Associazione Nazionale Imprese dell'Industria Congressuale).
Website: www.assointerpreti.it

Associazione Nazionale Italiana Traduttori e Interpreti (ANITI)

ANITI was founded in 1956 under the name of SNITI (Sindicato Nazionale Italiano Traduttori Interpreti). The official name was changed to ANIT in 1978.

Address:
Via Lambrate 10
20131 Milano
Italy
Phone: 39 022870336
Website: www.aniti.it

JAPAN

Japan Association of Translators (JAT)

The Japan Association of Translators (JAT) was founded in May 1985 as a means for individual translators to exchange information and insight, thereby helping each other not just to do a better job for their clients but a more rewarding one for themselves as well. In 2001 JAT became an incorporated non-profit organization under Japanese law. JAT membership is open to all individuals interested in Japanese/English and English/Japanese translation and interpretation. There are no particular professional qualifications necessary to join JAT.

Address:
2-19-15-808, Shibuya
Shibuya-ku
Tokyo 150-0002
Phone: (+81) 3 6644 0343
Website: www.jat.org

Japan Translation Federation Incorporated (JTF)

Japan Translation Federation is a non-profit industrial organization permitted by the Ministry of Economy, Trade and Industry. Its objectives are to promote translation businesses through the implementation of researches, studies, seminars, training of skilled persons and the participation in international conferences related to translation and to contribute thereby to the economic and social development of Japan

Contact Information:
Phone: 03-3555-6365
Website: www.jft.jp/

MEXICO

Asociación de Traductores e Intérpretes de Monterrey (ATIMAC)

ATIMAC is a non-profit organization which was organized in 1980 and formed in 1983.

Contact Information:
Phone: 528 183 58 71 21
Website: www.atimac.org.mx/

Asociación de Traductores Profesionales (ATP)

Address:
Bajio 335-104
Col. Roma Sur
06760 Mexico, D.F.
Mexico
Phone: 525 264 6787

Organización Mexicana de Traductores (OMT)

OMT was formed in 1992 in order to promote and support the translation and interpretation professions.

Address:
Capítulo Occidente
Av. Vallarta 1525-304
Col. Americana, Guadalajara
Jalisco – Mexico
Phone: 044-33-1398-2997
Website: www.omt.org.mx/

PERU

Asociación de Traductores Profesionales del Perú (ATPP)

ATPP is a private Association founded in Lima in 1992 with the objective to promote the translation and interpretation professions. To become a member, you must be a professional translator or interpreter with at least 10 years of experience in the field.

Address:
Casilla postal 18-0251
Lima 18
Peru
Website: www.atpp.org/esp

Colegio de Traductores del Perú (CTP)

CTP is an autonomous institution, comprised of professionals with a Degree in Translation or in Translation & Interpretation.

Address:
Av. Reducto 975
Urb. San Antonia
Lima 18 – Peru
Phone: (51-1) 242-1412
Website: www.colegiodetraductores.org.pe/

PORTUGAL

Associação Portuguesa de Tradutores (APT)

APT is the association for the defense of translators and the Portuguese language. It is a member of CEATL (European Council of Associations of Literary Translators) and AIETI (Iberic Association of Translation and Interpretation Studies).

Address:
R. de Ceuta
4/B, GAR.5
2795-056 Linda-a-Velha
Oeiras-Portugal
Phone: 96 45 89322
Website: www.apt.pt/

SPAIN

ACE Traductores (ACEtt)

ACEtt was founded in 1983 with the purpose of defending the interests and legal rights of literary translators. It is a founding member of CEATL (Consejo Europeo de Asociaciones de Traductores Literarios).

Address:
C/Santa Teresa, 2-3°
28004 Madrid
Spain
Phone: (34) 91-446-70-47
Website: www.acett.org

Asociación Aragonesa de Traductores e Intérpretes (ASATI)

ASATI is a non-profit Association founded in 2002 and comprised of translators and interpreters residing in Aragón.

Contact Information:
Website: www.asati.es

Asociación Galega de Profesionais da Traducción e da Interpretación (AGPTI)

Address:
Nebrixe, 4A
Bribes, 15659 Cambre
A Coruña, Galicia
Spain
Phone: (34) 986 48 10 12
Website: www.agpti.org/castelan/

Asociación Profesional Española de Traductores e Intérpretes (APETI)

APETI was founded in 1954. It has more than half a century of experience in promoting to the highest intellectual and ethical standards, the translation and intepretation professions. It is one of the first Associations of translators and interpreters, in the world.

Address:
Plaza de los Mostenses
1, 4ª planta
Oficina 2
28015 Madrid – España- Unión Europea
Phone: 34 915 410 723
Website: www.apeti.org.es/

SWITZERLAND

Arabic Translation and Intercultural Dialogue (ATIDA)

The Arabic Translation and Intercultural Dialogue Association (ATIDA) is working to bring together those who work in the field of translation from and into Arabic, and those who are interested in inter-cultural dialogue. ATIDA provides an e-portal that is designed to meet the needs of translators. ATIDA has a database containing details of translators whose mother tongue is Arabic, in order to facilitate obtaining work for them, and to provide them with other services that are compatible with ATIDA's mission. Additionally, ATIDA has forums where members can exchange and discuss ideas about any issue considered worthy.

Address :
P.O.Box 34
1211 Geneva 13 Switzerland
Website: www.atida.org

Association Suisse des Traducteurs Jurés (ASTJ)

ASTJ was founded in Geneva in 1995. It seeks to contribute to the promotion of the professional image of the sworn translators, to defend the interests of the sworn translators, and to also federate the sworn translators.

Contact information:
Website: www.astj.ch/

Association Suisse des Traducteurs, Terminologues et Interprètes (ASTTI)

ASTTI's objectives are to defend the professional interests of its members, to promote the profession and to collaborate with the translation schools in Switzerland.

Address:
Postgasse 17
3011 Berne
Switzwerland
Phone: 031 313 88 10
Website: www.astti.ch/

Localization Industry Standards Association (LISA)

Founded in 1990, LISA is the leading international forum for organizations doing business globally. LISA promotes the following global business values worldwide through its members: Global Responsibility; Global Entrepreneurship; Global Leadership; Global Cooperation. Some of the services provided by LISA to its members are: Consulting services for Globalization; Research and Publications; Networking Opportunities; Educational Opportunities; Technical and Business TouchPoint Advisories.

Address:
LISA's Headquarters is located in:
Domaine en Praël
CH-1323 Romainmôtier, Switzerland
Website : www.lisa.org

TAIWAN

Taiwan Association of Translation and Interpretation (TATI)

The Taiwan Association of Translation and Interpretation (TATI) was formally established on July 5, 1997 in Taipei.

Contact Information:
Website: http://www.tati.org.tw/

UKRAINE

Ukrainian Translators' Association (UTA)

Ukrainian Translators Association was founded in response to an overwhelming demand in the quality of translation and interpreting services.

The UTA members adhere to the code of professional conduct and are carefully vetted before admission into membership as full members.

Address:
39, Hogolivska St.
P.O. Box 18
UA – 04053
Kiev, Ukraine
Phone: (380 44) 244-61-61
Website: www.uta.org.ua

UNITED KINGDOM

Association of Translation Companies (ATC)

Founded in 1976, the ATC is, perhaps, one of oldest professional groups representing the interests of translation companies in the world. It is dedicated not only to representing the interests of translation companies, but also to serving the needs of translation purchasers. The Association of Translation Companies welcomes new members from around the world. Full membership is open to translation companies meeting ATC's criteria and operating in the UK. Overseas membership is available to translation companies operating everywhere else outside the UK.

Address:
Unit 28, Level 6 North
New England House
New England Street
Brighton BN1 4GH
Phone: 44(0) 1273 676777
Website: www.atc.org.uk

Chartered Institute of Linguists (IOL)

The Chartered Institute of Linguists serves the interests of professional linguists throughout the world and acts as a respected language assessment and accredited awarding body. Founded in 1910, the Institute now has around 6,500 Fellows, Members and Associate Members. It aims to: promote the learning and use of modern languages; improve the status of all professional linguists; establish and maintain high standards of work ; serve the interests of all linguists and ensure professional standards amongst language practitioners through its Code of Conduct.

Address:
Saxon House
48 Southwark Street
London, SE1 1UN
United Kingdom
Phone: 44 (0) 20 7940 3100
Website: www.iol.org.uk/

Hellenic Association of Translators & Interpreters (HATI)

HATI's objectives are: to form a representative body of practising professional translators and interpreters working with Greek as their SL or TL; to promote and maintain high standards of professional translation and interpreting with Greek as SL or TL; to arrange for professional examinations for translation and interpreting with Greek as SL or TL; to promote and protect the interests of practitioners and their clients in all matters relating to translating and interpreting with Greek as SL or TL; to establish rules and recommendations for Translators and Interpreters working with Greek as their SL or TL in all matters relating to their professional practice and to ensure that members abide by the Association's code of practice; to provide opportunities for practitioners to get together, correspond, exchange ideas, develop their skills and knowledge, and generally to help in the acquisition and dissemination of knowledge relating to their profession; to promote the translation into English of literary texts written in Greek; to do all lawful things relevant to furthering the objects of the Association.

Address:
16-18 Paddington Street
London W1U 5AS
United Kingdom
Phone: 44 (0) 20 88155811
Website: www.hati.org.uk/

The Institute of Translation and Interpreting (ITI)

The Institute of Translation & Interpreting was founded in 1986 as the only independent professional association of practicing translators and interpreters in the United Kingdom. It is now one of the primary sources of information on these services to government, industry, the media and the general public. With its aim of promoting the highest standards in the profession, ITI serves as a meeting place for all those who understand the importance of translation and interpreting to the economy and society, particularly with the expansion of a single European market of over forty languages and the growth of worldwide communications. ITI offers guidance to those entering the profession and advice not only to those who offer language services but also to their customers. ITI has a large and growing international membership of translators and interpreters, not just in the United Kingdom but also in continental Europe and other countries where English is commonly used. ITI offers a number of services to its members and to non-members. Some of those services include: an arbitration service; a referral service; 24 hour Legal Helpline; advice on continuing professional development; networking opportunities; a public information system.

Address:
The Institute of Translation and Interpreting (ITI)
Fortuna House
South Fifth Street
Milton Keynes
MK9 2EU
United Kingdom
Phone: 44 (0) 1908 325250
Website: www.iti.org.uk

The Translators' Association (TTA)

A constituent part of the Society of Authors, TTA was set up in 1958 to provide translators with an effective means of protecting their interests and sharing their concerns. Since then it has brought about Public Lending Right for translators, developed a model publishing agreement, which is used widely, and continues to raise awareness of the translating profession. The TA is a source of expert advice, a representative for individuals, and an advocate for the profession as a whole, with its own Committee and decision-making structure. The Benefits of being a member of TTA include: Contract vetting: confidential clause by clause advice on contracts; advice and support on professional issues; meetings and workshops on literary and professional topics, and social events. The TA is part of the Society of Authors. To join you must have one full-length work, or its equivalent, published or accepted for publication.

Address:
84 Drayton Gardens
London SW 10 9SB
United Kingdom
Phone: 020 7373 6642
Website: www.societyofauthors.org/subsidiary_groups/translators_association

UNITED STATES

American Translators Association (ATA)

The American Translators Association (ATA), founded in 1959, is a professional association founded to advance the translation and interpreting professions and foster the professional development of individual translators and interpreters. Its 10,000 members in more than 90 countries include translators, interpreters, teachers, project managers, web and software developers, language company owners, hospitals, universities, and government agencies. Association membership is available to individuals (Active, Corresponding, Associate, Student) and organizations (Corporate, Institutional).

Contact Information:
American Translators Association
225 Reinekers Lane, Suite 590
Alexandria, VA 22314
Phone: (703) 683-6100
Website: www.atanet.org

ATA CHAPTERS

Atlanta Association of Interpreters and Translators (AAIT)
P.O. Box 12172
Atlanta, GA 30355
Phone: (404) 729-4036
Website: www.aait.org

Carolina Association of Translators and Interpreters (CATI)
125 Windsor Circle
Chapel Hill, NC 27516
Phone: (919) 577-0840
Website: www.catiweb.org

Delaware Valley Translators Association (DVTA)
606 John Anthony Drive
West Chester, PA 19382
Website: www.dvta.org

Michigan Translators/Interpreters Network (MiTiN)
P.O. Box 852
Novi, MI 48376-0852
Phone: (248) 344-0909
Website: www.mitinweb.org

Mid-America Chapter of ATA (MICATA)
6600 NW Sweetbriar Lane
Kansas City, MO 64151
Phone: (816) 741-9441
Website: www.ata-micata.org

Midwest Association of Translators and Interpreters (MATI)
Indiana University-Purdue University
Dept of World Languages & Cultures
425 University Boulevard
Indianapolis, IN 46202
Phone: (317) 274-8957
Website: www.matiata.org

**National Capital Area Chapter
of ATA (NCATA)**
P.O. Box 5757
Washington, DC 20016-5757
Phone: (703) 255-9290
Website: www.ncata.org

New York Circle of Translators (NYCT)
P.O. Box 4051
Grand Central Station
New York, NY 10163-4051
Phone: (212) 334-3060
Website: www.nyctranslators.org

Northeast Ohio Translators Association (NOTA)
33425 Bainbridge Road
Solon, OH 44139
Phone: (440) 519-0161
Website: www.notatranslators.org

Northern California Translators Association (NCTA)
P.O. Box 14015
Berkeley, CA 94712-5015
Phone: (510) 845-8712
www.ncta.org

Northwest Translators and Interpreters Society (NOTIS)
1037 NE 65th Street, Suite 107
Seattle, WA 98115
Phone: (206) 701-9183
Website: www.notisnet.org

Upper Midwest Translators and Interpreters Association (UMTIA)
701 Park Avenue
Minneapolis, MN 55415
Phone: (612) 873-8591
Website: www.umtia.com

The American Association of Language Specialists (TAALS)
TAALS is an international professional association of interpreters and translators working at the international level, either at conferences or in permanent organizations, and determines their qualifications and standards.

Contact Information:
The American Association of Language Specialists
(TAALS)
P.O. Box 39339
Washington, D.C. 20016
Website: www.taals.net

American Literary Translators Association (ALTA)

Mailing Address:
The University of Texas at Dallas
800 W. Campbell Rd, Mail Station JO51
Richardson, TX 75080-3021
Website: www.utdallas.edu/alta

The California Court Interpreter Association (CCIA)
The California Court Interpreters Association (CCIA) is a non-profit organization dedicated to advancing the standards of court interpreting and furthering the interests of the profession. It was founded in 1971, and now has chapters throughout California, as well as members-at-large in many states of the Union and in other countries. Nearly 800 members provide the various court systems plus the medical and business communities with expert interpreting and translating in approximately 70 languages and dialects. Membership in the CCIA is open to all those employed in, interested in, or concerned with the profession of court interpreting.

Address:
The California Court Interpreter Association (CCIA)
P.O. Box 2454
Orangevale, CA 95662
Website: www.ccia.org

The National Association of Judiciary Interpreters and Translators (NAJIT)

The National Association of Judiciary Interpreters and Translators (NAJIT) is a professional association that was first chartered as a non-profit organization under the New York State Laws and was incorporated as the Court Interpreters and Translators Association, Inc. (CITA) in 1978. NAJIT seeks to promote quality interpretation and translation within the judicial system. It has over 1200 members including practicing interpreters, translators, educators, researchers, students and administrators. Most of its members are located in the United States; however, it has members in Latin America, in Europe, in Asia and in Australia.

Address:
The National Association of Judiciary Interpreters and Translators
1707 L Street, NW
Suite 570
Washington, DC 20036
Phone: (202) 293-0342
Website: www.najit.org

Washington State Court Interpreters and Translators Society (WITS)

The Washington State Court Interpreters and Translators Society is a non-profit, professional organization officially established in the State of Washington in September 1988. WITS seeks to further the goals of the interpreting and translating profession, enhance the professional standing of our members and inform the public about our profession.

The purpose of WITS is to unite court interpreters, translators, and those having an interest in this field into a society which represents their professional ideas and interests, in accordance with the Washington State Code of Conduct for Court Interpreters; to provide continuing education for its members; to promote general awareness of the role of the interpreter and translator.

Address
Washington State Court Interpreters and Translators Society
PO Box 1012
Seattle, WA 98111-1012
Phone: (206) 382-5690
Website: www.witsnet.org

URUGUAY

Colegio de Traductores Públicos del Uruguay (CTPU)

CTPU's objectives are to represent its members, defend its members' interests, establish relationships with national and foreign institutions that are comprised of professional translators and interpreters, establish relationships with legal and literary institutions as well as universities.

Address:
Colonia 892
Piso 6, esc. 604
Montevideo 11.100
Uruguay
Phone: (598-2) 903 31 30
Website: www.colegiotraductores.org.uy/

REFERENCE MATERIALS

Accounting Software

As a business owner and even a freelancer, you will be responsible for preparing invoices, recording payments, and compiling your company's financial information. This plays a major role in determining the success or failure of your company. Luckily, we have access to a wide range of affordable and efficient accounting software to assist us in performing these tasks. However, as we all know too well, every year we find ourselves with the options of upgrading our software.

When choosing an accounting software, be sure to evaluate your company's size, in addition to your needs. There is a good selection of Accounting Software that is tailored to the different needs of a small or large business. Be sure to research what each product offers and determine which one is beneficial to you at that particular point in time. When you consider which accounting software to buy, I recommend you buy with a 1 to 2 year projection in mind. In other words, buy the product knowing that it will last you for at least 1 to 2 years. When you are starting out, be careful not to buy a product that is too expensive, under the assumption that the more expensive it is, the more efficient it will be. That is not always the case. Most of the accounting software out there are pretty efficient. A good way to determine which one you should buy is to review their information online, download or order a sample version for practice, and be sure to ask your colleagues and friends what they like about their accounting software. Your accountant is another good source of reference.

Another important point about accounting software is to be sure that whoever will be using the software (if it's you or one of your employees), that person must have a pretty good understanding and knowledge of basic accounting concepts and principles. Keying in the information is simple, however, one must know how to properly enter the information. Keep in mind that your accounting software will only reflect the information or data entered by the person. This can definitely create a major problem leading to erroneous financial reports. Make sure that in addition to using the tutorial or sample software, if you do not have any former background in accounting, that you invest the time and money (if necessary) in getting the necessary training to efficiently use the program. This is the financial future of your company you are dealing with.

Another thing to look for when choosing your accounting software is to make sure the software will have no problem running with other software you currently have, such as Microsoft Word, Excel, or Access. Also, know if the software you purchase is widely used among accountants or accounting firms. This will be helpful when you have to submit your financial data or backup files to your CPA for the preparation of financial reports and during tax filing season.

It's important to also know how many people will be using the software. In other words, how many licensed user(s) will there be? This information will determine which software package to buy.

Don't feel pressured into upgrading your software every year. I recommend you consider upgrading when your needs have changed and that you have outgrown your current software.

Remember when deciding on which accounting software to buy, this involves making a business decision. As you do for any other types of business decision, you need to think about the costs and benefits involved. Which product should you buy that will bring you the higher return on your investment? This is the question you must ask yourself, when in doubt.

For the past four years, I have been using QuickBooks (Intuit product) Premier Professional Services Edition. I have been very pleased with it. However, there are other products on the market as well. You should do your research to determine which one will best suit your needs.

Here is a Partial List of Accounting Products.

Those software products are tailored for various users. From the self-employed starting out, from the small business with less than 4 employees to the medium to large businesses with several hundred employees and even with multiple office locations. Be sure to check their respective websites or to contact them in order to determine which specific product suits your needs. Some of them allow you to download a free trial of their product prior to purchasing.

Intuit was founded in 1983. Intuit's products include Quicken, Quickbooks and TurboTax tailored for small businesses and personal finances and with versions for PC and Mac. It also offers international software versions for Australia, Canada, Germany, Hong Kong, New Zealand, Singapore, South Africa and Thailand. Please visit their website at www.intuit.com for more information on their specific products.

Microsoft Office Accounting Express 2008 is an essential tool for managing your home-based business. It is a user friendly software that allows you to create quotes, invoices, and receipts; write checks, track your expenses, reconcile online bank accounts. It also offers additional features. For more information visit their website at www.office.microsoft.com.

Sage Software's main focus is to provide business management software and services to small and medium-sized businesses. It serves customers in the United States and Canada. Some of Sage Software's products include the following:

Simply Accounting Entrepreneur which helps start-up, small and home-based businesses perform entry-level accounting tasks easily and efficiently. Their direct website is www.simplyaccounting.com

Peachtree Complete Accounting is ideal for small businesses. Please visit their direct website at www.peachtree.com for more information.

Peachtree Quantum is a business accounting software that supports up to 10 users (local and remote). For more information visit their website at www.peachtreequantum.com or contact their one of their specialists in the U.S at 1-800-871-1735.

For more information about Sage Software, visit their website at www.sagesoftware.com.

MYOB Premier Accounting 2008

MYOB is a small business accounting and management software for Mac and Windows platforms. MYOB is an international provider offering business solutions in Australia, China, Hong Kong, Ireland, Malaysia, New Zealand, Singapore, United Kindgom and the United States. Please visit their website at www.myob.com or contact them in the United States at 1-800-322-6962.

ADDITIONAL SOFTWARE

Translation Office 3000 is an Accounting and Administrative Software for Freelance Translators and Translation Agencies. Translation Office 3000 is an advanced accounting tool that easily and seamlessly integrates into the business life of professional freelance translators. This program will be your personal accountant, adviser, assistant, and project manager. Translation Office 3000 transforms the complex and diverse world of the translation business into a manageable concept implemented in software. This organizational tool was designed to help translators track and manage many translation jobs from many clients around the world.

TO3000 is very flexible and created with freelance translators in mind. It is no problem to have a client database with different currencies, prices, and services. Translation Office 3000 is one powerful tool with which it is easy to organize all aspects of freelance translation work. TO3000 will save you time on each stage of your translation work and will show you a complete picture of your translation business. TO3000 offers a user-friendly interface. You also have the opportunity to try this software for freelance translators for 30 days absolutely free of charge.

For more information about this product, visit their website at http://www.to3000.com.

Useful links to Accounting Buying Guides:
www.accountingsoftwareadvisor.com
www.findaccountingsoftware.com
http://accounting-software-review.toptenreviews.com

ENGLISH MONOLINGUAL DICTIONARIES (PARTIAL LIST)

21st Century Dictionary of Slang, by Watts, Karen, ISBN 044021551X

Browser's Dictionary of Foreign Words & Phrases, by Varchaver, Mary & Moore, Frank, L., ISBN 0471383724

Cambridge International Dictionary of Phrasal Verbs, by Cambridge University Press, ISBN 0521565588

Dictionary of American Slang, by Chapman, Robert L. & Kipfer, Barbara A., ISBN 006117646X

Merriam-Webster's Dictionary of English Usage, by Merriam-Webster, ISBN 0877791325

The American Heritage Dictionary, by Houghton Mifflin Company, ISBN 0618701729

Webster's Third New International Dictionary – Unabridged, by Merriam-Webster, ISBN 0877792011

BUSINESS AND FINANCE

Dictionary of Finance and Investment Terms, by Downes, John & Goodman, Jordan E., ISBN 0764134167 – Barron's Business Dictionaries Series

Dictionary of International Economics & Finance Terms, by Clark, John, ISBN 0852976852

Dictionary of International Business Terms, by Capela, John J., & Hartman, Stephen W. ISBN 9780764124457 – Barron's Business Guides Series

CIVIL ENGINEERING AND CONSTRUCTION

The Wiley Dictionary of Civil Engineering and Constructions, by Webster, L.F, Webster, Len, Webster Robert Ed., ISBN 0471181153

LEGAL

Black's Handbook of Criminal Law Terms, by Garner Bryan A., ISBN 0314243224

Black's Law Dictionary, by Garner, Bryan A., ISBN 0314152342

Dictionary of Criminal Justice Terms, by Gould Publications Staff, ISBN 0875262767

Dictionary of Modern Legal Usage, by Garner, Bryan A., ISBN 0195142365

Law Dictionary, by Gifis, Steven H. ISBN 9780764119965 – Barron's Legal Guides Series

MEDICAL

American Psychiatric Glossary, by Shahrokh, Narriman C. & Hales, Robert E., ISBN 1585621463

Dorland's Illustrated Medical Dictionary, by Newman W. Dorland, ISBN 141602364X

Stedman's Medical Abbreviations, Acronyms & Symbols, by Stedman's Staff, ISBN 0781772613

Stedman's Medical Dictionary, by Stedman, ISBN 0781733901

ENGLISH PRACTICAL REFERENCES

A Practical Guide to Localization, by Esselink, Bert, ISBN 1588110060

A Practical Guide for Translators, by Samuelsson-Brown, Geoffrey, ISBN 1853597295

AMA Manual of Style, by JAMA and Archives Journal, ISBN 0195176332

Barron's 1001 Pitfalls in English Grammar, by Hopper, Vincent F, Craig, R.P., ISBN 0812037197

Copyediting – A Practical Guide, by Judd, Karen, ISBN 1560526084

Elements of Legal Style, by Garner, Bryan A., ISBN 019514628

Mark my Words – Introduction and Practice in Proofreading, by Smith, Peggy, ISBN 0935012230

Oxford American Writer's Thesaurus, by Lindberg, Christine, McKean, Erin, ISBN 0195170768

Routledge Encyclopedia of Translation Studies, by Baker, Mona, ISBN 0415255171

The Chicago Manual of Style, by University of Chicago, ISBN 0226104036

The Languages of the World, by Katzner, Kenneth, ISBN 0415250048

The Translator (Novel), by Crowley, J., ISBN 0380815370

ONLINE REFERENCES

* Please note that when using any online bilingual dictionaries, you must be very careful and be certain that you take into account the context before rushing to use the translation provided online.

www.acronymfinder.com – a comprehensive online dictionary of acronyms, abbreviations, initialisms. It contains more than 4 million acronyms and abbreviations.

www.wordreference.com – free online translation dictionaries. Most popular languages are French, Spanish, Italian.

www.alphadictionary.com – an online resource providing access to online dictionaries in over 200 languages.

www.proz.com – an online site which provides tools and opportunities for translators, translation companies and others in the language industry, to network, expand their businesses and improve their work.

www.atanet.org – the official website of the American Translators Association (ATA)

www.najit.org – the official website of the National Association of Judiciary Interpreters and Translators (NAJIT)

BOOK STORES IN CANADA, FRANCE, UNITED KINGDOM AND UNITED STATES (PARTIAL LIST)

CANADA

Librairie Michel Fortin
3714, St. Denis Street
Montréal, Quebec H2X3L7, Canada
Phone: 514-849-0845
Toll Free: 877-849-5719
Website: www.librairiemichelfortin.com

Renaud-Bray
Various Locations
Website: www.renaud-bray.com
Phone in Montreal: 514-276-7651

FRANCE

La Maison du dictionnaire
98, Bd du Montparnasse
F-75014 PARIS
FRANCE
Phone : +33 (0) 1 43 22 12 93
Website: www.dicoland.com

Librairie Eyrolles
61, boulevard St. Germain
75005 Paris
Phone: 33 (1) 44 41 41 87
Website: www.eyrolles.com

UNITED KINGDOM

Oxford University Press
Several locations in the United Kingdom
Phone for Customer Service (Direct Orders): 44 (0) 1536 741727
Website: www.oup.co.uk

UNITED STATES

EducaVision
Educavision's main focus to is the designing, developing and publishing of Haitian-related educational materials.
7550 NW 47th Avenue
Coconut Creek, FL 33073
Phone: 954-968-7433
Website: www.educavision.com

French and European Publications Inc.
610 Fifth Avenue
New York, NY 10020
Phone: 212-581-8810
Website: www.frencheuropean.com

InTrans Book Service
Contact: Freek Lankhof
P.O. Box 467
Kinderhook, NY 12106
Phone: 518-758-1755
Website: www.intransbooks.com

Libreri Mapou
Libreri Mapou is considered to be the largest Haitian Bookstore in Miami, Florida.
5919 NE 2nd Avenue
Miami, FL 33137
Phone: 305-757-9922
Website: www.librerimapou.com

Pierre Books
2340 Hollywood Blvd
Hollywood, FL 33020
Phone: 954-924-1660
Toll Free: 1-888-702-0766
Website: www.pierrebooks.com

Schreiber Publishing, Inc.
P.O. Box 4193
Rockville, MD 20849
Phone: 301-424-7737
Toll Free: 800-822-3213
Website: www.schreiberpublishing.com

ONLINE BOOKSTORES

www.amazon.com
www.amazon.ca
www.amazon.fr
www.borders.com
www.barnesandnoble.com
www.powells.com
www.booksamillion.com
www.bookshop.blackwell.co.uk
www.harvard.com
www.abc.nl

CLOSING REMARKS

It has been a pleasure for me to write this book. I certainly hope that you have enjoyed reading it as well.

I want to point out that the information in this book is not intended to provide legal, financial or business advice. Please be sure to consult a lawyer, an accountant, and even a business consultant, when making business decisions. I, along with my editors, have made great effort in reviewing and proofreading the content of this book for errors; however, I want to emphasize that we are not to be held liable for any errors or information that have been omitted in this book. Furthermore, we are not to be held liable either for any decision or action that may be taken based on information in this book.

Throughout this book, I have provided product and material references; please note that this in no way signifies that I am advocating for a specific product. I have not had the opportunity to try all of the products and/ or reference materials listed in this book. In cases where I have had a direct experience with a product or reference material, I have mentioned it clearly. Throughout the book, I have also provided website links for specific information or organizations relating to translation and interpreting. In most instances, the weblinks start off with (www.), if for some reason, you are not able to access the link as stated in this book, please include (http://) in front of the (www.). Keep in mind that you are encouraged to do your own research and obtain the relevant information that is necessary to assist you in making the right product or reference material choice.

As of the time of publication of this book, all information and references provided were accurate and up to date.

Once again, I wish you great success in your professional translation career!

Sincerely,
Carline Férailleur-Dumoulin

Partial List Of Translation And Interpreting Schools (U. S. And Abroad)

ALGERIA

Université d'Alger
Faculté des Lettres et des Langues
Département de Traduction et Interprétation
Address: 2, Rue Didouche Mourad, Alger
Phone: 21321 637834
Website: www.univ-alger.dz

Université d'Oran Es-Siéna
Institut de Langues Etrangères
Département de Traduction et d'Interprétariat
Address: El-M'nouar
Oran, Algeria
31000
Phone: 213.6.33.77.44 / 213.6.41.69.67

ARGENTINA

Instituto Nacional de Educación Superior No. 28 "Olga Cossettini," Rosario
Address: Sarmiento 2902
Rosario, Sante Fe
Phone: 0341-4728675/76
Website: www.iesoc.com.ar

Instituto de Enseñanza Superior en Lenguas Vivas "Juan Ramón Fernández"
Carlos Pellegrini 1515
1011 Buenos Aires
Argentina
Phone: 4322-3992/3996/3998

Pontificia Universidad Católica Argentina Santa María de los Buenos Aires
Facultad de Filosofía y Letras Traductor Público en Idioma Inglés
Address: Av. Alicia M. de Justo 1500
Buenos Aires 1107
Argentina
Phone: (54-11) 4-349-0444 /0290 /91/92
Website: www.uca.edu.ar

Universidad Adventista del Plata
Facultad de Humanidades
Educacion y Ciencias y Ciencias Sociales
25 de Mayo 99
(3103) Libertador San Martín entre Ríos
Argentina
Phone: 00 54 343 4918000
Website: www.uapar.edu

Universidad del Salvador
Facultad de Filosofía y Letras
Address: Tucuman 1699
C1020ADM

Ciudad Autonoma de Buenos Aires
Argentina
Phone: (54-11) 4374-3816 / 4375-2958
Website: www.salvador.edu.ar

Universidad de Buenos Aires
Facultad de Derecho y Ciencias Sociales
Address: Viamonte 430 st.
Buenos Aires City
Argentina
Phone: (054) 011.4510.1100
Website: www.uba.ar

Universidad de Belgrano
Facultad de Lenguas y Estudios Extranjeros
Address: Zabala 1837
(C1426DQG) Capital Federal
Argentina
Phone: 54-11-4788-5400
Website: www.ub.edu.ar

Universidad de Morón
Facultad de Informática
Ciencias de la Comunicación y Técnicas Especiales
Address: Cabildo 134
(B1708JP) Morón, Buenos Aires
Argentina
Phone: (54-11) 5627-2000
Website: www.unimoron.edu.ar

Universidad del Museo Social Argentino
Escuela Universitaria de Lenguas / Facultad de Lenguas Modernas
Address: Av. Corrientes 1723
C1042AAD
Ciudad Autónoma de Buenos Aires
Argentina
Phone: (54-11) 4375-4601

Universidad Nacional de Catamarca
Facultad de Humanidades
Phone: (03833) 424099
Website: www.unca.edu.ar

Universidad Nacional de Córdoba
Facultad de Lenguas
Phone: 4334065/66
Website: www.unc.edu.ar

Universidad Nacional de La Plata
Facultad de Humanidades y de Ciencias de la Educación
Departamento de Lenguas Modernas
Avda 7 No. 776
1900, La Plata, Buenos Aires
Argentina
Phone: 4230128/4236669/4230125/4236673
Website: www.unlp.edu.ar

AUSTRALIA

Adelaide Institute of Training and Further Education (TAFE)
20 Light Square. Adelaide SA 5064
Phone: 61.8.2078269

Deakin University
Faculty of Arts
School of Languages, Interpreting and Translating
Phone: 1300 334 733
Website: www.deakin.edu.au

Edith Cowan University
Faculty of Education and Arts
Lawley Campus
Phone: (61 8) 6304 0000
Website: www.ecu.edu.au

Macquarie University
Division of Linguistics & Psychology
Department of Linguistics
Center for Translation and Interpreting Research
NSW 2109
Australia
Phone: 61 2 9850 7111
Website: www.mq.au

Royal Melbourne Institute of Technology
Institute of Training and Further Education
Translating and Interpreting Studies
Address: GPO BOX 2476V
Melbourne VIC 3001
Australia
Phone: 61 3 9925 2000
Website: www.rmit.edu.au

Southbank Institute of Technology
Mailing Address: Locked Mail Bag 14
South Brisbane QLD4101
Phone: 07 3244 5117
Website: www.southbank.edu.au

University of New England
University Campus
11 Hills Beach Road
Biddeford, ME 04005
Phone: (207) 283-0171
Website: www.une.edu

University of New South Wales
Faculty of Arts and Social Sciences
School of Languages and Linguistics
Address: NSW 2052
Australia
Phone: 61 2 9385 1000
Website: www.unsw.edu.au

University of Queensland
Department of Japanese and Chinese Studies
Brisbane QLD 4072 Australia
Phone: 61 7 3381 1111
Website: www.uq.edu.au

University of Western Sydney
College of Arts
Interpreting and Translation
Address: Locked Bag 1797
Penrith South DC
NSW 1797
Phone: 61 2 9852 5222
Website: www.uws.edu.au

AUSTRIA

Universität Graz
Institut für Theoretische und Angewandte Translationswissenschaft
Address: Merangasse 70/1
8010 Graz
Phone: 43/316/380-2666
Website: www.kfunigraz.ac.at/

Universität Innsbruck
Institut für Translationswissenschaft
Main Address: Christoph-Probst-Platz
Innrain 52
A-6020 Innsbruck
Phone: +43(0) 512-507-4250
Website: www.uibk.ac.at/

University of Vienna / Universität Wien
Translation Studies
Main Address: Dr. Karl-Lueger-Ring 1
1010 Vienna
Austria
Phone: 43-1-4277-0
Website: www.univie.ac.at/

BELARUS

Minsk State Linguistic University
Department of Interpreting and Translation
Address: 21 Zakharov Street
Minsk, 220062
Republic of Belarus
Phone: 375172-331562

BELGIUM

Centre Européen de Traduction Littéraire (CETL)
Institut Supérieur de Traducteurs et Interprètes de la Communauté
française de Belgique (I.S.T.I.)
34, rue Joseph Hazard - 1180 Bruxelles (Uccle)
Belgique
Phone: 32 2569 68 12

Erasmushogeschool
Address: Nijverheidskaai 170
B-1070 Brussel
Phone: 32 (0) 2 523 37
Website: www.ehb.be

Institut Cooremans
Ecole Supérieure de Traducteurs et d'Interprètes
Address: Place Anneessens 11
1000 Bruxelles
Phone: (32) 2 551 02 16
Website: http://www.brunette.brucity.be/ferrer/cooremans/index.html

Institut Libre Marie Haps
Address: ILMH asbl
Rue d'Arlon 11
1050 Bruxelles
Phone: 02/793.40.00
Website: www.ilmh.be

Institut Supérieur de Traducteurs et Interprètes
Address: ISTI, Haute Ecole de Bruxelles
Rue Joseph Hazard, 34
B-1180 Bruxelles
Phone: 02/340 1280
Website: www.heb.be/isti

Universitè de Mons-Hainaut
Faculté de Traduction et Interprétation
Address: 17, Avenue du Champ de Mars
7000 Mons
Phone: 065-37-36-01
Website: www.umh.ac.be

BRAZIL

Centro Universitario Iberoamericano (UNIBERO)
Av. Brigadeiro Luís Antônio
871 CEP: 01317-001
Sâo Paulo, SP
Phone: 0800 941 4444
Website: http://www.ibero.br/

Pontifícia Universidade Católica de Rio de Janeiro (PUC-RIO)
Rua Marques Sâo Vicente 225
Rio de Janeiro, RJ
Brazil, 22453-900
Phone: 55 (21) 3114 1134
Website: www.puc-rio.br/

Pontifícia Universidade Católica de São Paulo (PUC-SP)
Rua Monte Alegre 984
São Paulo, SP
Brasil 05014-901
Phone: 55 (11) 3670 8000
Website: www.pucsp.br/

Universidade Castelo Branco (UCB)
Avenida Santa Cruz 1631
Rio de Janeiro, RJ
Brasil
21710-250
Phone: 55 (21) 2406 7700
Website: www.castelobranco.br/

Universidade Cidade de São Paulo (UNICID)
Rua Cesario Galeno 448/475 – Tahuapé
São Paulo, SP
CEP 03071-000
Phone: 55 (11) 2178-1212
Website: www.unicid.br/

Universidade de São Paulo. Centro Interdepartamental de Tradução e Terminologia (USP-CITRAT)
Av. Professor Luciano Gualberto
403- Sala 267A
Cid. Universitária
CEP-05508-900
São Paulo, SP
Brasil
Phone: 55 (011) 3091-3674
Website: http://www.fflch.usp.br/citrat/citrat.htm

119

Universidade Estadual de Campinas (UNICAMP)
Departamento de Lingüística Aplicada
Programa de Pós-Graduação
C.P. 6045. IEL. UNICAMP. 13081-970. Campinas. S.P.
Phone: 55.192.398241
Website: www.unicamp.br/

Universidade Federal de Juiz de Fora
Departamento de Letras Estrangeiras Modernas
Rua Benjamin Constant
790. 36015-400 Juiz de Fora. MG
Phone: 55. 32.299 3150
Website: www.ufjf.br/

Universidade Federal Fluminense
Instituto de Letras
Av. Visconde de Rio Branco
s/n. (Campus Gragoatá)
24.210-130 Niterói, Rio de Janeiro
Phone: 55.21.7174082
Website: www.uff.br/

Universidade Mackenzie
Faculdade de Letras
Educacao e Psicologia
Rua Itambé 45
Higienópolis 01239-902
São Paulo, SP
Phone: 55 11 236 8393
Website: www.mackenzie.br/

CANADA

Concordia University
Address: 1455 De Maisonneuve Blvd. West
Montreal, Quebec, Canada H3G 1M8
Phone: 514-848-2424
Website: www.concordia.ca

McGill University
Centre for Continuing Education
Translation Studies
Address: 845 Sherbrooke St.
W. Montréal, Québec, Canada H3A 2T5
Phone: 514-398-1484
Website: www.mcgill.ca

Queen's University
Mailing Address: 99, University Avenue
Kingston, Ontario CA K7L 3N6
Phone: 613-533-2000
Website: www.queensu.ca

Université Laval
Département de langues, linguistique et traduction
Address: Faculté des lettres
Pavillon Charles-De-Koninck, Bureau 2289
Université Laval, Quebec, Canada G1K7P4
Phone: 418-656-3263
Website: www.lli.ulaval.ca

Université de Moncton
Département de Traduction et des Langues
Faculté des Arts et des Sciences Sociales
Address: Moncton (Nouveau-Brunswick)
Canada E14 3E9
Phone: 506-858-4214
Website: www.umoncton.ca

Université de Montréal
Faculté des Arts et des Sciences
Département de Linguistique et Traduction
Address: Pavillon Lionel Groulx
3150, rue Jean-Brillant
Montreal, Quebec
Canada H3T 1N8
Phone: 514-343-6111
Website: www.umontreal.com

Université du Québec
Main Address: 475, rue du Parvis
Québec,(Québec)
G1K 9H7
Phone: 418-657-3551
Website: www.uquebec.ca

University of British Columbia
Department of French, Hispanic and Italian Studies
Address: #797 – 1873 East Mall
Vancouver, British Columbia
Canada V6T 1Z1
Phone: 604-822-2879
Website: www.ubc.ca

University of Ottawa
School of Translation and Interpretation
Address: Arts Hall
70 Laurier Avenue East
Room 401
Ottawa, ON
Canada K1N 6N5
Phone: 613-562-5719
Website: www.uottawa.ca

CHILE

Escuela Americana de Traductores e Intérpretes (EATRI)
Address: Avenida Condell 451
Providencia, Santiago
Chile
Phone: 223-1089 / 225-8018
Website: www.eatri.cl

Instituto Profesional ELADI
Address: José M. Infante 927
Providencia, Santiago
Chile
Phone: 56.2 204 85 73
Website: http://eladi.cl/

Pontificia Universidad Católica de Chile
Facultad de Letras
Address: Av. Libertador Bernardo O'Higgins 340
Santiago, Chile
Phone: (56 2) 3542000
Website: www.uc.cl/

Universidad Católica de Valparaíso
Facultad de Filosofía y Educación
Address: Avenida Brasil 2950
Valparaiso, Chile
Phone: (56) (32) 227 3000
Website: www.pucv.cl/

Universidad de Concepción
Facultad de Humanidades y Arte
Address: Victor Lamas 1290
Casilla 160-C
Concepción, Octava
Región, Chile
Phone: (56-41) 220 40 00

CHINA

Beijing Foreign Studies University (Bei Wai)
Address: Oberseas Students Affairs
2 North Xisanhuan Avenue
Beijing, 100089, P.R. China
Phone: 0086 10 88816549/88810671
Website: www.bfsu.edu.cn

Beijing International Studies University (BISU)
Address: Beijing International Studies University
China 100024
Phone: 86-10-65778481
Website: www.bisu.edu.cn/english /
www.bisu.edu.cn/

Beijing No. 2 Foreign Language Institute
(also known as Second Foreign Translation Institute)
Address: 1, Dingfuzhuang. Chaoyang District. Beijing 100024
Phone: 86.10.576772

China Foreign Affairs University
Department of English & International Studies
(formerly Foreign Affairs College)
Address: 24 Zhanlan Road, West District, Beijing 100037
Phone: 86-10-68323896

Shanghai International Studies University
Graduate Institute of Interpretation and Translation
Address: 550 Dalian Xilu, Shanghai 200083
Phone: (+8621) 6561.0046
Website: http://giit.shisu.edu.cn

Sichuan International Studies University
Address: Postgraduate Faculty
Shapingba, Chongqing, 400031
Phone: 86 23 6538 5296
Tianjin Normal University
Foreign Languages Department
Translation Studies Program
Address: Ba Li Tai. Tianjin 300074
Phone: 86.22.3345024
Xiamen University
Foreign Languages Department
Address: Xiamen. Fujian
Phone: 86.592.2086380

COLOMBIA

Colegio Mayor de Bolivar
Calle de la Factoria No. 34-29
Cartagena, Colombia
Phone: 57 (5) 664 4060

Corporación Universitaria de Colombia Ideas
Campuses in Itagui, Quibdo, Arauca, and Santa Fe de Bogotá
Calle 70 No 10-75
Santafe de Bogotá, Colombia
Phone: (091) 255 83 21
Website: www.ideas.edu.co/

Politécnico Colombo Andino
Facultad de Lenguas Modernas
Avenida 19 No 3-16 Of. 218
Bogotá, Colombia
Phone: (091) 282 77 98
Website: www.polcolan.edu.co/

Universidad Autónoma de Manizales
Departamento de Lenguas Extranjeras
Antigua Estacion del Ferrocarril
P. O. Box 441
Manizales, Colombia
Phone: (968) 81 04 50 or 81 02 90
Website: www.autonoma.edu.co/

Universidad Jorge Tadeo Lozano
Seccional del Caribe (Cartagena de Indias)
Departamento de Humanidades
Calle de la Chichería # 38-42
Cartagena de Indias, Colombia
Phone.: +57(5) 655 4000 / 664 8534

Universidad Nacional de Colombia (CUTRA)
Facultad de Ciencias Humanas
Area Curricular de Ciencias del Lenguaje
Departamento de Lingüística
Ciudad Universitaria
Transversal 38-A No. 40-04
Edificion "Uriel Gutiérrez"
Bogotá D.C., Colombia
Phone: 57 (1) 316-5000
Website: www.unal.edu.co/

Universidad Santiago de Cali
Carrera 62 x Calle 5 Barrio Pampa Linda
P. O. Box 4102 Cali.
Cali, Colombia
Website: www.usc.edu.c

CROATIA

University of Zagreb
Faculty of Humanities and Social Sciences
Address: Ivana Lucića 3
HR- 10000 Zagreb
Phone: 385 1 61 20 111
Website: www.unizg.hr/

CUBA

Alianza Francesa de Cuba
Address: Calle J #302 esquina a 15
Verdado La Habana
Phone: (53) 7 833 3370
Website: http://es/afcuba.org/

Centro de Lingüística Aplicada
Address: Calle 9 Nr. 253 entre 10 y 12
Reparto Vista Alegre
Santiago de Cuba, Cuba C.P. 90400
Phone: 53-22-643507/646418/642760

CZECH REPUBLIC

Charles University
Institute of Translation Studies
Address: Charles University in Prague
Information and Advisory Center
Celetna 13
116 36, Praha 1
Phone: (+420) 224 491 850
Website: www.cuni.cz

DENMARK

Aarhus School of Administration
Department of Language and Business Communications
Address: Aarhus School of Business
University of Aarhus
Fuglesangs Allé 4
DK – 8210 Aarhus V.
Phone: 45 89 48 66 88
Website: www.asb.dk/

The Copenhagen Business School
Faculty of Modern Languages
Address: Solbjerg Plads 3
DK – 2000 Frederiksberg
Phone: 45 3815 3815
Website: http://uk.cbs.dk/

University of Copenhagen
Department of English, Germanic and Romance Studies
The Translation Center
Address: Faculty of Humanities
Njalsgade 128
DK-2300
Phone: 45 3532 2626
Website: www.ku.dk/

EGYPT

Al-Alsun University
Khalifa Al-Maamoun Street
Abassya - Cairo, Egypt
Phone: 2626259
Website: www.als.shams.edu.eg/

The American University
Center for Adult and Continuing Education
Arabic and Translation Studies Division
28, Falaki St. Bab El-Louk
P.O. Box 2511
Cairo, Egypt
Phone: (202) 797-6872
Website: www.aucegypt.edu/

FINLAND

University of Joensuu
Savonlinna Language Institute
5, P.O. Box 126
FI 57101, Savonlinna
Phone: (358) (0) 15 511 7755
Website: www.joensuu.fi

University of Tampere
School of Modern Languages and Translation Studies
33014 University of Tampere
Finland
Phone: 358 3 3551 6150
Website: www.uta.fi/

University of Turku
School of Classical and Romance Languages
FI- 20014 University of Turku
Phone: 358 2 333 8700
Website: www.utu.fi/

University of Helsinki
Department of Translation Studies
P.O. Box 94
45101 Kouvola
Finland
Phone: 358 (0) 9-1 911
Website: www.helsinki.fi/university/

University of Vaasa
Department of Modern Finnish and Translation
P.O. Box 700
FI – 65101 Vaasa
Phone: 358 (6) 324-8111
Website: www.uwasa.fi/

FRANCE

Ecole Superieure de Traducteurs et d'Interpretes (ESIT)
Address: École Supérieure d'Interprètes et de Traducteurs
Centre Universitaire Dauphine
75775 Paris cedex 16
FRANCE
Phone: (33) 01-44-05-42-05
Website: www.esit.univ-paris3.fr

Institut Superieur d'Interpretariat et de Traduction (ISIT)
Address: ISIT
12 rue Cassette - 75006 PARIS
Phone: 33 (0) 1 42 22 33 16
Website: www.isit-paris.fr

Université Charles de Gaulle – Lille 3
Adress: Université Charles-de-Gaulle - Lille 3
Domaine universitaire du "Pont de Bois"
rue du Barreau - BP 60149
59653 Villeneuve d'Ascq Cedex
Phone : 33 (0) 3 20 41 60 00
Website: www.univ-lille3.fr/

Université de Haute-Alsace
Département des Langues et Affaires
Address: UHA - Faculté
Campus Fonderie
16 rue de la Fonderie
F-68093 MULHOUSE CEDEX
Phone : 33 (0) 3 89 56 82 03
Website: www.fsesj.uha.fr/

Université de Nice - Sophia Antipolis
Département des Arts, Lettres et Langues
Address: Grand Château
28 avenue Valrose
BP 2135
06103 Nice Cedex 2
Phone: 04 92 07 60 60
Website: http://lettres.unice.fr/

Université de Pau et des Pays de l'Adour (UPPA)
Faculté des Lettres, Langues et Sciences humaines
Address: Av. de l'université'BP 576
64012 PAU cedex
Phone: 33 (0) 5 59 40 70 00
Website: www.univ-pau.fr

Université de Toulouse II- Le Mirail
Address: 5 allées Antonio Machado
31058 TOULOUSE Cedex 9
Phone: (33) 5 61 50 42 50
Website: http://w3.univ-tlse2.fr/

Université d'Orléans
Faculté des Lettres, Langues et Sciences Humaines
Address: UFR Lettres, Langues et Sciences Humaines
10 Rue de Tours - BP 46527 - 45065 ORLEANS Cedex 2
Phone : 33 (0) 2-38-41-71-06
Website: www.univ-orleans.fr/lettres

Université Marc Bloch
Institut de Traducteurs, d'Interprètes et de Relations Internationales
(ITI-RI)
Address: ITI-RI
22 Rue René Descartes
BP 80010
67084 Strasbourg cedex
France
Phone: 33 (0) 3 88 41 74 86
Website: www.itiri.com

Université Sorbonne Nouvelle – Paris 3
Address: Ecole Supérieure d'Interprètes et de Traducteurs - ESIT
Place du Maréchal-de-Lattre-de-Tassigny
75116 Paris
Website: www.univ-paris3.fr/

GERMANY

Humboldt Universität zu Berlin
Unter den Linden
6. PSF 1297
D-10099 Berlin
Germany
Phone: 49.30.2093 21 69
Website: www.hu-berlin.de/

Universität Bonn
Adenauerallee 102
D-53113 Bonn
Germany
Phone: 49.228.73 84 15
Website: www1.uni-bonn.de/

Cologne University of Applied Sciences /Fachhochschule Köln
Faculty of Information Studies and Communication Sciences
Mainzerstraße 5
D-50678 Köln
Phone: 49 (0) 221 8275 3376
Website: www.fh-koeln.de/

Johannes Gutenberg-Universität Mainz in Germersheim
Fachbereich Angewandte Sprach-und Kulturwissenschaft
Address: An der Hochschule, 2. D-76711 Germersheim
Phone: 49.72.74 50 80
Website: www.uni-mainz.de/

Martin-Luther-Universität Halle-Wittenberg
Address: Nietlebenerstraße, 10. D-06126 Halle
Phone: 49.345.648 143
Website: www.uni-halle.de/

Hochschule Magdeburg – Stendal (FH)
University of Applied Sciences
Address: Haus 1
Breitscheidstr. 2
39114 Magdeburg
Phone: 49.391. 88 64 249
Website: http://www.fachkommunikation.hs-magdeburg.de

GREECE

Centre for English Language and Training
Address: 77 Academias Street
106 78 Athens
Greece
Phone: 0030 210 330 2406 / 1455
Website: www.celt.edu.gr/

Metafrasi School of Translation Studies
Address: 52 Akadimias
10679 Athens
Greece
Phone: 03210 36 29 000
Website: www.metafrasi.edu.gr/

The Ionian University
Department of Foreign Languages. Translation and Interpretating
Address: Megaro Kapodistria
Corfu 49100
Greece
Phone: 26610-87200
Website: www.ionio.gr/

GUATEMALA

Escuela Profesional de Traducción e Interpretación
Address: Torre Pradera
Oficina 1004
Zona 10
Guatemala City, Guatemal
Phone: (502) 2367-0232
Website: www.epti-translation.com

HONG KONG

Caritas Francis Hsu College
Department of Language Studies
Address: 2-16 Caine Road
Hong Kong
Phone: (852) 2521 4693
Website: www.cfhc.caritas.edu.hk/

Chinese University of Hong Kong (CUHK)
Faculty of Arts
Address: Shatin, NT
Hong Kong SAR
The People's Republic of China
Phone: (852) 2609 8951
Website: www.cuhk.edu.hk/

City University of Hong Kong
Department of Chinese, Translation and Linguistics
Mailing Address: Tat Chee Avenue
Kowloon
Hong Kong SAR
Phone: (852) 2788 7654
Website: www.cityu.edu.hk/
Lingnan University
Department of Translation

Address: 8 Castle Peak Road
Tuen Mun, New Territories
Phone (General Inquiries): 852 2616 8888
Website: www.LN.edu.hk/

The University of Hong Kong
Faculty of Arts
Mailing Address: Pok Fu Lam Road
Hong Kong
Phone (General Inquiries) : 852 2859 2111
Website: www.hku.hk/

HUNGARY

Eötvös Loránd University (ELTE)
Faculty of Humanities
Address: 1088 Budapest
Múzeum krt. 4/A
Hungary
Phone: 36 1 411 6700
Website: www.elte.hu/

University of Debrecen
Center of Arts, Humanities & Sciences
Address: Office of the President
University of Debrecen
H-4010 Debrecen
P.O. Box 95
Hungary
Phone: 36-52-518-655
Direct Link: www.englishstudies.sci.unideb.hu/
Website: www.unideb.hu/

University of Pécs
Faculty of Humanities
Address: H-7624 Pécs
Ifjúság útja 6
Hungary
Phone: 36-72/503-600/4126
Website: www.ki.pte.hu/

INDIA

Bangalore University
Faculty of Arts
Address: Jnana Bharathi Campus
Jnana Bharathi Post
Bangalore – 560 056
Karntaka, India
Phone: 080-22961006
Website: www.bub.ernet.in/

University of Hyderabad
School of Humanities
P.O. Central University
Hyderabad – 500 046
A.P., India
Phone: 23132102-23132103
Website: www.uohyd.ernet.in/

INDONESIA

University of Indonesia
Faculty of Humanities
Address: Universitas Indonesia
UI Depok Campus 16424
Indonesia
Phone: 62-21-786 7 222
Website: www.ui.edu

IRAQ

Al-Mustansiriyah University
College of Arts
Phone: (964) 415 0429
Website: www.uomustansiriyah.edu.iq/

IRELAND

Dublin City University (DCU)
Faculty of Humanities & Social Sciences
Address: Dublin 9
Ireland
Phone: 353 (0) 1 700 500
Website: www.dcu.ie/

ISRAEL

Bar-Ilan University
The Faculty of Humanities
Translation and Interpreting Studies
Mailing Address: Bar-Ilan University
Ramat Gan
52900 Israel
Phone: 972-3-531-8111
Website: www1.biu.ac.il/

ITALY

Istituto Superiore Interpreti Traduttori (ISIT)
Language Department
Address: Via Alex Visconti, 18
20151 Milan
Italy
Phone: (39) 02 339 12081
Website: www.scuolecivichemilano.it/

Istituto Superiore per Interpreti e Traduttori (ISIT)
Address: Via Roma, 256
I-81024 Maddaloni (Caserta)
Italia
Phone: (39) 823.40 31 23
Website: www.ssmlmaddaloni.it/

Scuola Superiore di Studi Universitari per Interpretati e Traduttori di Torino
Address: Via Secondo, 35
Torino
Italia
Phone: (39) 011/59 54 90

Scuola Superiore per Interpreti e Traduttori GB Vico
Address: Via Sabotino
11. I-21200 Varese
Italia
Phone: (39) 0332.23 73 04

SSML Gregorio VII
Address: Via Gregorio VII
N 126
00165- Rome
Italy
Phone: (39) 6 639 0300
Website: www.gregoriosettimo.eu

Università di Bologna
Scuola Superiore di Lingue Moderne per Interpreti e Traduttori
Address: Corso della Repubblica, 136
I-47100 Forlì
Italia
Phone: (39) 543-45 02 75
Website: www.ssit.unibo.it/

Università degli Studi di Trieste
Scuola Superiore di Lingue Moderne per Interpreti e Traduttori
Address: Via Fabio Filzi 14
I-34132 Trieste
Italia
Phone: (39) 040 558 2300
Website: www.sslmit.univ.trieste.it/

Università di Lecce
Facolta di Lingue e Lett. Straniere
Address: Edificio ex-sperimentaletabacchi
Via Calasso
(73100) Lecce
Italia
Phone: (39) 0832-306049
Website: www.lingue.unile.it/

JAPAN

Daito Bunka University
Graduate School of Economics
Address: Daito Bunka University International Center
1-9-1, Takashimadaira
Itabashi-ku
Tokyo, Japan 175-8571
Phone: 03-5399-7323
Website: www2.daito.ac.jp/en/

Inter School
Address: 8-5-32 Akasaka Minato-ku
Tokyo, Japan 107
Phone: 81.3.3479.4861
Website: www.interschool.jp/

International Christian University
Address: 10-2 Osawa 3-chome
Mitaka-shi
Tokyo, Japan 181
Phone: 81-422-33-3038
Website: www.icu.ac.jp/

Kyoto Tachibana Women's University
Address: 34 Yamada-cho
Oyake
Yamashina-ku
Kyoto, Japan 607
Phone: 81-75-571-1111
Website: www.tashibama-u.ac/jp/english

Osaka University of Foreign Studies
Address: 1-1 Yamadaoka
Suita
Osaka, Japan 565-0871
Phone: 81-6-6879-7103
Website: www.osaka-u.ac.jp/eng/

Toyo Eiwa Women's University
Address: 32-1 Miho-cho
Midori-ku
Yokohama-shi
Kanazawa, Japan 226
Phone: 81.45-922-5511
Website: www.toyoeiwa.ac.jp/

JORDAN

University of Jordan
Address: Amman 11942 Jordan
Phone: 962.6 535 5000
Website: www.ju.edu.jo/

KOREA

Hankuk University of Foreign Studies
Address: 270 Imun-dong
Dongdaemun-Gu
Seoul 130-791 Korea
Phone: 82 (2) 2173-2063
Website: www.hufs.ac.kr/user/hufsenglish/

LATVIA

University of Latvia
Faculty of Modern Languages
Address: 19 Raina Blvd
Riga
LV 1586 Latvia
Phone: 371.67034.334 (Intl relations Dept.)
Website: www.lu.lv/eng/

LEBANON

Notre Dame University
Faculty of Humanities
Address: Main Campus
P.O. Box 72
Zouk Mikael
Zouk Mosbeh, Lebanon
Phone: 961-9 218950
Website: www.ndu.edu.lb/

Université Saint-Joseph
Institute of Languages and Translation
Address: Damascus Road
BP 17-5208 Mar Mikhaël
Beirut 1104-2020
Lebanon
Phone: 961 (1) 421 000
Website: www.usj.edu.lb/

Université de Saint-Esprit de Kaslik (USEK)
Holy Spirit University
Faculté des Lettres
Address: Main Campus
Jounieh P.O.B. 446
Mount Lebanon, Lebanon
Phone: 961 (9) 600 000
Website: www.usek.edu.lb/

MEXICO

Instituto Superior de Interpretes y Traductores
Address: Río Rhin No. 40
Col. Cuauhtémoc
C.P. 06500
México, D.F.
Phone: 55 66 77 22
Website: www.isit.edu.mx/

Universidad Autonoma de Baja California
Facultad de Idioma Ensenada
Address: Boulevard Zertuche y Boulevard de los Lagos S/N
Fracc. Valle Dorado
C.P. 22890
Ensenada
Baja California, México
Phone: 52 (646) 175-0740
Website: www.uabc.mx/

Universidad Autónoma de Tlaxcala
Facultad de Filosofía y Letras
Address: Carretera a Ocotlan S/N
Tlaxcala, México
Phone: (01246) 465 27 00
Website: www.uatx.mx/

Universidad Intercontinental
Address: Cantera 251
Tlalpan, México
Phone: (55) 5487 1300
Website: www.uic.edu.mx/

MOROCCO

École Supérieure Roi Fahd de Traduction
(The King Fahd School of Translation)
Address: B.P. 410
Tanger, Maroc
Phone: 039 94 28 13
Website: www.ecoleroifahd.uae.ma/

NETHERLANDS

Hogeschool West-Nederland
Hogeschool West-Nederland voor Vertaler en Tolk
(West-Netherlands University of Applied Sciences for Translation and Interpreting)
Address: The Hague
Netherlands
Website: www.west-nederland.nl/

Universiteit van Amsterdam
University of Amsterdam
Address: Spui 21
1012 WX Amsterdam
The Netherlands
Phone: 31 20 525 9111
Website: www.uva.nl/

Universiteit Utrecht
Utrecht University
Faculteit der Letteren
Address: Faculty of Humanities
Kromme Nieuwegracht 46
3512 HJ Utrecht
The Netherlands
Phone: 31 (0) 30 253 6105
Website: www.uu.nl/

NEW ZEALAND

Auckland Institute of Technology
School of Languages
Mailing Address: General Course Inquiry
Private Bag 92006
Auckland 1142
New Zealand
Phone: 09 921 9909
Website: www.aut.ac.nz/

The University of Auckland
Faculty of Arts
Mailing Address: Private Bag 92019
Auckland Mail Center
Auckland 1142
New Zealand
Phone: 64 9 373 7599 ext 85060
Website: www.auckland.ac.nz/

NORWAY

Universitetet I Agder
Agder University
Faculty of Humanities and Education
Mailing Address: Service Box 422

NO-4604
Kristiansand, Norway
Phone: 47 38 14 10 00
Website: www.uia.no/en

PERU

Universidad Ricardo Palma
Ricardo Palma University
Facultad de Humanidades y Lenguas Modernas
Address: Av. Benavides 5440
Santiago de Surco
Lima 33 – Peru
Apto Postal 1801
Phone: (0511) 708-0000
Website: www.urp.edu.pe/

Universidad Femenina del Sagrado Corazón (UNIFE)
Programa de Traducción e Interpretación
Address: Av. Los Frutales 954
Urb. Camacho La Molina
Peru
Phone: (0511) 436-4641
Website: www.unife.edu.pe/

POLAND

Uniwersytet Im. Adama Mickiewicza W Posnaniu
Adam Mickiewicz University
Faculty of Modern Languages and Literature
Address: H. Wieniawskiego 1
61-712 Poznán, Poland
Phone: (48-61) 829 4308
Website: http://www.guide.amu.edu.pl/

Carline Férailleur-Dumoulin

Akademia Polonisjna w Częstochowie
Polonia University in Czestochowa
Address: Polinia University
Ul. Pulaskiego 4/6
42-200 Czestochowa
Phone: 48 (034) 3684226
Website: www.ap.edu.pl/

Uniwersytet Jagiellonski
Jagiellonian University
Faculty of Philology
Address: ul, Golebia 24
31-007 Krakow
Phone: (48 12) 422-10-33
Website: www.uj.edu.pl/

Uniwersytet Łódzki
University of Lodz
Center for Translation Studies
Address: ul. Narutowicza 65
90-131 Lodz, Poland
Phone: (48 42) 635-42-36
Website: www.uni.lodz.pl/

Uniwersytetu Warszawskiego / University of Warsaw
Instytut Lingwistyki Stosowanej / Institute of Applied Linguistics
Address: Instytut Lingwistyki Stosowanej UW
Ul. Browarna 8/10
00-311 Warsawa, Poland
Phone: 48 22 552 09 21
Website: www.ils.uw.edu.pl/

PORTUGAL

Escola Superior de Tecnologia e Gestão do Instituto Politécnico de Leiria
Address: Campus 2
Morro do Lena
Alto do Vierio
2411-901 Leiria
Apartado 4163
Phone: 244 820300
Website: http://www.estg.ipleiria.pt

Instituto Superior de Assistentes e Intérpretes, Porto
Address: Rua do Campo Alegre, 1376.
P-4150-175 Porto
Portugal
Phone: 351 22 609 92 04

Universidade Autónoma de Lisboa
Address: Palácio dos Condes do Redondo
Rua de Santa Marta, No. 56
1169-023 Lisboa
Portugal
Phone: 800 291 291
Website: http://www.universidade-autonoma.pt/

Universidade de Coimbra
Faculdade de Letras
Address: Praça da Porta Férrea
P-3000 Coimbra
Portugal
Phone: 039-25551
Website: http://uc.pt/

Universidade de Lisboa
Address: Alameda Universidade
Cidade Universitária
1649-004 Lisboa
Portugal
Phone: 351 217 967 624
Website: http://www.ul.pt/

Universidade do Minho
Address: Largo do Paço
4704-553 Braga
Portugal
Phone: 253 604110
Website: http://www.uminho.pt/

Universidade do Porto
Faculdade de Letras
Address: Via Panorâmica, s/n
4150-564 Porto
Portugal
Phone: 351 22 607 7100
Website: http://www.up.pt/

ROMANIA

Babes-Bolyai University/Universtatea BABEŞ-BOLYAI
Department of Applied Modern Languages
Address: Universitatea BABEŞ-BOLYAI
Mihail Kogălniceanu nr. 1 RO
400084 Cluj-Napoca
Phone: 40 264 40 53 00
Website: http://www.ubbcluj.ro/

RUSSIA

Linguistic University of Nizhny Novgorod
Address: 31-A Minin Street
Nizhny Novgorod
603155 Russia
Phone: 7 (831) 4362 049
Website: http://www.dia.lunn.ru/

Perm State University
Address: 15 Bukireva str.
Perm, Russia 614990
Phone: 7 (3422) 396407
Website: http://www.psu.ru/

St. Petersburg State University
Address: 7-9 Universitetskaya nab.
St. Petersburg
199034 Russia
Phone: 7 812 3282000
Website: http://www.www.spbu.ru/e/

SAUDI ARABIA

King Saud University
Address: King Saud University
BOX 2454
Riyadh 11451
Kingdom of Saudi Arabia
Phone: 966 (1) 467-0112
Website: http://www.ksu.edu.sa/

SLOVAKIA

Comenius University
Faculty of Philosophy
Address: Kancelaria rektora
Rektorat UK
Safarikovo nam. 6
818 06 Bratislava 16
Slovakia
Phone: 421 2 5292 1594
Website: http://www.univa.sk/

Univerzita Konštantína Filozofa v Nitre/Constantine The Philosopher University in Nitra
Faculty of Arts
Address: Tr. A. Hlinku 1
SK – 949 74 Nitra
Slovakia
Phone: 421 37 6408 111
Website: http://www.ukf.sk/

SOUTH AFRICA

University of Johannesburg
Address: PO Box 524
Auckland Park
2006 South Africa
Phone: 27 (0) 11 559 2911
Website: http://www.uj.ac.za/

University of South Africa
Department of Linguistics
Section Translation Studies
Mailing Address: PO Box 392
UNISA 0003
South Africa
Phone: 27 11 670 9000
Website: http://www.unisa.ac.za/

University of Stellenbosch
Address: Private Bag X1
Matieland
7602 stellenbosch
South Africa
Phone: 27 21 808 9111
Website: http://www/sun.ac.za/

University of the Witwatersrand
Address: Private Bag 3
WITS Johannesburg 2050
South Africa
Phone: 27 0 (11) 717 1000
Website: http://www.wits.ac.za/

SPAIN

Universidad Alfonso X el Sabio
Facultad de Lenguas Aplicadas
Address: Universidad Alfonso X el Sabio
La Universidad de la Empresa
Campus de Vilanueva de la Cañada
Madrid
Phone: (34) 902 100 868
Website: www.uax.es/

Universidad de Alicante
Facultad de Filosofía y Letras
Address: Edificio B
08193 Bellaterra (Cerdanyola del Vallès)
Barcelona
Phone: (34) 935811558
Website: www.uab.es/
Direct Link: www.lletres.uab.cat/

Universidad de Castilla-La Mancha

Escuela de Traductores de Toledo
Plaza de Santa Isabel, 5
45071 Toledo
España
Phone: (34) 925 223 729
Website: www.uclm.es/

Universidad de Granada

Departamento de Traducción e Interpretación
Address: C/Buensuceso
11 Granada
C.P. 18002
Granada
Phone: (34) 958 244106
Website: www.ugr.es/

Universidad de Las Palmas de Gran Canaria

Facultad de Traducción e Interpretación
Phone: (34) 928 451 700
Website: www.ulpgc.es/

Universidad de Málaga

Facultad de Filosofía y Letras
Address: Campus de Teatinos
29071 Málaga
Phone: (34) 952 13 34 19
Website: www.uma.es/

Universidad de Salamanca

Facultad de Traducción y Documentación
Address: C/Francisco Vitoria 6-16
Salamanca
España 37008
Phone: (34) 923 294 580
Website: http://exlibris.usal.es/

Universidade de Vigo
Departamento de Traducción e Lingüítica
Address: Facultad de Filoloxia e Traducción – Vigo
E-36200 Vigo
Phone: (34) 86 812 371
Website: www.webs.uvigo.es/

Universidad Pontificia Comillas
Facultad de Ciencias Humanas Y Sociales
Address: C/Alberto Aguilera 23
28015 Madrid
Phone: (34) 91 542 2800
Website: www.upcomillas.es/

Universitat Pompeu Fabra
Facultat de Traducció i Interpretació
Address: La Rambla, 30-32
08002 Barcelona
Phone: 93 542 22 42
Website: www.upf.edu/factii/

SWEDEN

Stockholm University / Stockholms Universitet
Institute for Translation and Interpretation Studies
(Tolk- och översättarinstitutet)
Address: SE-106 91 Stockholm
Sweden
Phone: 46 8 16 20 00
Website: www.su.se/

Carline Férailleur-Dumoulin

SWITZERLAND

University of Geneva / Université de Genève
Ecole de Traduction et d'Interprétation
Address: Université de Genève
24 rue du Général-Dufour
CH-1211 Genève 4
Phone: (41) 0 22 379 71 11
Website: www.unige.ch/

TAIWAN

Fu Jen Catholic University
Address: 510 Chung Cheng Rd
Hsinchuang
Taipei County
2405 Taiwan
Republic of China
Phone: 886-2-29052000
Website: http://www.fju.edu.tw/

National Taiwan Normal University (NTNU)
Graduate Institute of Translation and Interpretation
Address: 162, HePing East Road
Section 1
Taipei, Taiwan
Website: http://www.ntnu.edu.tw/

THAILAND

Burapha University
Address: 169 Long-Hard Bangsaen Road
Tambon Saenooh
Amphur Muang
Chonburi
20131 Thailand
Phone: 66-3810-2222
Website: http://www.buu.ac.th/

Chulalongkorn University
Address: 254 Phyathai Road
Patumwan
Bangkok, Thailand 10330
Phone: 662-215-0871-3
Website: http://www.chula.ac.th/

Ramkhamhaeng University
Address: Ramkhamhaeng Road
Hua Mark
Bangkapi
Bangkok, Thailand 10240
Phone: 662-310-8000
Website: http://www.ru.ac.th/

Thammasat University
Address: 2 Prachan Road
Bangkok
10200 Thailand
Phone: 66 (0) 2613 3333
Website: http://www.tu.ac.th/

TURKEY

Bilkent University
Address: 06800 Bilkent
Ankara, Turkey
Phone: 90 312 290 4000
Website: http://www.bilkent.edu.tr/

Bogaziçi University
Address: 34342 Bebek
Istanbul, Turkey
Phone: 0212 359 5400
Website: http://www/boun.edu.tr/

Hacettepe University
Address: 06532 Ankara
Turkey
Phone: (90) 312 305 5000
Website: http://www.hacettepe.edu.tr/

Istanbul University
Address: Istanbul Universitesi
Center Campus
34452 Beyazit
Eminonu – Istanbul
Turkey
Phone: 0 (212) 440 00 00
Website: http://www.istanbul.edu.tr/

UKRAINE

Karazin Kharkiv National University
Address: 4 Svobody sq.
61077 Kharkiv
Ukraine
Phone: 38 (057) 705 12 47
Website: http://www.univer.kharkov.ua/

UNITED KINGDOM

Aston University
Languages & Social Sciences
Address: Aston Triangle
Birmingham B47ET
Phone: 0121 204 3700
Website: www1.aston.ac.uk/

Middlesex University
School of Arts & Education Courses
Modern Languages & Translation Studies
Address: The Burroughs
London
NW4 4BT
Phone: 44 (0) 20 8411 5000
Website: www.mdx.ac.uk/

Newcastle University
School of Modern Languages
Address: Old Library Building
Newcastle University
Newcastle upon Tyne
NE1 7RU United Kingdom
Phone: 44 (0) 191 222 7441
Website: www.ncl.ac.uk/

University of Birmingham
Centre for English Language Studies (CELS)
Address: Centre for English Language Studies
Westmere House
University of Birmingham
Edgbaston
Birmingham
B15 2TT
United Kingdom
Phone: 44 (0) 121 414 5695 / 6
Website: www.cels.bham.ac.uk/

University of Leeds
School of Modern Languages and Cultures
Centre for Translation Studies
Address: University of Leeds
School of Modern Languages and Cultures
Leeds LS2 9JT
United Kingdom
Phone: 44 (0) 113 343 3234
Website: www.leeds.ac.uk/

157

University of Surrey
Department of Languages and Translation Studies
Address: Faculty of Arts & Human Sciences
Department of Languages and Translation Studies
University of Surrey
Guildford
Surrey
GU2 7XH
United Kingdom
Phone: 01483 68622
Website: www.surrey.ac.uk/

University of Warwick
The Centre for Translation and Comparative Cultural Studies
Address: The Centre for Translation and Comparative Cultural Studies
Coventry
CV4 7AL
United Kingdom
Phone: 44 (0) 24 7652 3655
Website: www2.warwick.ac.uk/

UNITED STATES

ARIZONA
Arizona State University
College of Liberal Arts and Sciences
Address: University Drive and Mill Avenue
Tempe, AZ 85287
Phone: (480) 965-9011
Website: http://www.asu.edu/tempe/

Pima Community College
Certificate in Translation Studies (Spanish)
Associates of Applied Science (AA)
in Translation and Interpretation (Spanish)
4905 E. Broadway Blvd

Tucson, AZ 85709-1010
Phone: (520) 206-4500
Website: http://www.pima.edu

University of Arizona
P.O. Box 210432
Tucson, AZ 85721-0432
Phone: (520) 621-3615
Website: http://ncitrp.web.arizona.edu/

ARKANSAS
University of Arkansas
The Arkansas Programs in Creative Writing & Translation
Address: Program in Creative Writing and Translation
Department of English
333 Kimpel Hall
University of Arkansas
Fayetteville, AR 72701
Phone: (479) 575-4301
Website: www.uark.edu/

CALIFORNIA
California State University
Division of Extended Education
Certificate Program in Legal Interpretation
And Translation
5151 State University Drive
Los Angeles, CA 90032-8619
Contact: Joann Edmond
Phone: (323) 343-4900
Website: www.calstate.edu

Monterrey Institute of International Studies
Graduate School of Translation and Interpretation
Address: 460 Pierce Street
Monterey, CA 93940
Phone: (831) 647-4123
Website: http://translate.miis.edu/

National Hispanic University
Certificate Program in Translation and Interpretation
14271 Story Road
San Jose, CA 95127
Contact: George Guim
Phone: (408) 273-2765
Website: http://www.nhu.edu

National University
Mailing Address: 11255 North Torrey Pines Rd
La Jolla, CA 92037
Phone: (800) 628-8648
Website: http:///www.nu.edu/

San Diego State University
Address: 5500 Campanile Drive
San Diego, CA 92182
Phone: (619) 594-5200
Website: http://www.sdsu.edu/

Southern California School of Interpretation
Address: Santa Fe Springs, CA 90670
Phone: 800-625-6222
   (562) 906 9787
Website: http://www.interpreting.com/

Stanford University
Address: 450 Serra Mall
Stanford, CA 94305
Phone: (650) 723-2300
Website: http://www.stanford.edu

University of California
Professional Certificate in Translation and Interpretation (Spanish/English)
Address: UCLA Extension
10995 Le Conte Avenue
Los Angeles, CA 90024-2883
Phone: (310) 825-9082
Website: www.uclaextension.edu/

COLORADO
University of Denver
School of Professional and Continuing Studies
Address: University of Denver
University College
2211 South Josephine
Denver, CO 80208
Phone: (303) 871-3155
Website: http://www.universitycollege.du.edu

FLORIDA
Miami Dade College
Inter American Campus
Translation and Interpretation Studies
Address: 627 SW 27th Avenue
Miami, FL 33135-2937
Phone: (305) 237-8888
Website: http://www.mdc.edu/

Florida A&M University
Address: Tallahassee, FL 32307
Phone: (850) 599-3000
Website: http://www.famu.edu

Florida International University
Department of Modern Languages
Translation and Interpretation Program
Phone: (305) 348-2000
Website: http://w3.fiu.edu/translation/

University of Florida
Translation Studies
Address: 319 Grinter Hall
Gainesville, FL 32611-5530
Phone: (352) 258-6910
Website: http://www.ufl.edu/

GEORGIA
Georgia State University
Translation and Interpretation Program
Department of Modern and Classical Languages
Mailing Address: PO Box 3965
Atlanta, GA 30302-3965
Phone: (404) 413-2000
Website: http://www.gsu.edu/

HAWAII
University of Hawaii at Manoa
College of Languages, Linguistics and Literature
Center for Interpretation and Translation Studies
Address: 2500 Campus Road
Honolulu, HI 96822
Phone: (808) 956-8111
Website: http://www.uhm.hawaii.edu/

ILLINOIS
Northern Illinois University
Department of Foreign Languages and Literatures
Address: 1425 W Lincoln Hwy
DeKalb, IL 60115-2825
Phone: (815) 753-1000
Direct Link: http://www.forlangs.net
Website: http://www.niu.edu/

University of Illinois at Urbana Champaign
Continuing Education
Address: 302 E John Street
Suite 202
Champaign, IL 61820 MC 433
Phone: (877) 455-2687
Website: http://www.uiuc.edu

INDIANA
Indiana University
Department of Comparative Literature
Translation Studies (Specialization: Literary Translation)
Address: Indiana University
Department of Comparative Literature
Ballantine Hall 914
1020 E. Kirkwood Ave.
Bloomington, IN 47405-7103
Phone: (812) 855-7070
Website: http://www.indiana.edu

Rose-Hulman Institute of Technology
Department of Humanities and Social Services
Addres: 5500 Wabash Avenue
Terre Haute, IN 47803
Phone: (812) 877-1511
Website: http://www.rose-hulman.edu/

IOWA
University of Iowa
Department of Comparative Literature
Address: Iowa City, IA 52242
Phone: (319) 335-0330
Website: http://www.uiowa.edu

MARYLAND
University of Maryland
Address: 8400 Baltimore Avenue
Suite 100
College Park, MD 20742-5415
Phone: (301) 405-1000
Website: http://www.umd.edu/

MASSACHUSETTS
**Boston University Center for
Professional Education**
Community, Legal and Medical Interpreter
Certificate Program
1010 Commonwealth Avenue
Boston, MA 02215
**Effective January 2008, they've expanded
their program to offer interpreter training
in Vietnamese**
Phone: (617) 353-4497
University of Massachusetts
Translation Center at Amherst
Phone: (413) 545-0111
Website: www.umasstranslation.com

MICHIGAN
Marygrove College
Address: 8425 W. McNichols
Detroit, MI 48221
Phone: (313) 927-1200
Website: http://www.marygrove.edu

Oakland University
Department of Modern Languages & Literatures
Address: 418 Wilson Hall
Rochester, MI 48309-4401
Phone: (248) 370-2060
Website: http://www2.oakland.edu

Western Michigan University
Department of Foreign Languages
Summer Translation Institute (STI)
Address: Western Michigan University
Department of Foreign Languages
4th Floor
Sprau Tower
Kalamazoo, MI 49008-5338
Phone: (269) 387-3001
Website: http://www.wmich.edu

MINNESOTA
St. Olaf College
Address: 1520 St Olaf Avenue
Northfield, MN 55057
Phone: (800) 800-3025; (507) 786-3813
Website: http://www.stolaf.edu

NEBRASKA
University of Nebraska
Department of Modern Languages
Translation and Interpretation Program
Address: The University of Nebraska at Kearney
905 West 25ᵗʰ Street
Kearney, NE 68849
Phone: (308) 865-8441
Website: http://www.nebraska.edu/

NEW JERSEY
Montclair State University
College of Humanities and Social Services
Address: Montclair State University
Monclair, NJ 07043
Phone: (973) 655-4000
Website: http://www.montclair.edu

Rutgers University
School of Arts & Sciences
Department of Spanish and Portuguese
Address: Department of Spanish and Portuguese
105 George St
New Brunswick, NJ 08901-1414
Phone: (732) 932-9323
Direct Link: http://span-port.rutgers.edu
Website: http://www.rutgers.edu

NEW YORK
Binghamton University
(State University of New York, SUNY)
Translation Research and Instruction Program
Library Tower 1302
P.O. Box 6000
Binghamton, NY 13902-6000
Phone: (607) 777-2000
Email: http://trip@binghamton.edu

Brooklyn College
The City University of New York (CUNY)
Modern Languages & Literatures
Address: 4239 Boylan Hall
2900 Bedford Avenue
Brooklyn NY 11210
Phone: (718) 954-5451
Website: http://www.brooklyn.cuny.edu

Columbia University
Barnard College
Department of French
Address: 320 Milbank Hall
Barnard College
3009 Broadway
New York, NY 10027
Phone: (212) 854-8312
Website: http://www.barnard.columbia.edu

Hunter College
The City University of New York (CUNY)
Address: 695 Park Avenue
New York, NY 10065
Phone: (212) 772-4000
Website: http://www.hunter.cuny.edu

Marymount Manhattan College
Address: 221 East 71st Street
New York, NY 10021-4597
Phone: (212) 517-0564
Website: http://www.mmm.edu

Queens College
The City University of New York (CUNY)
Address: 65-30 Kissena Blvd
Flushing, NY 11367
Phone: (718) 997-5000
Website: http://www.qc.cuny.edu

New York University
School of Continuing and Professional Studies
Address: New York University
School of Continuing and Professional Studies
145 4th Avenue
Room 201
New York, NY 10003
Phone: (212) 998-7200
Website: www.scps.nyu.edu/

NORTH CAROLINA
Wake Forest University
Language Resource Center
Address: Wake Forest University
1834 Wake Forest Road
Winston-Salem, NC 27106
Phone: (336) 758-5000
Website: http://lrc.wfu.edu/

OHIO
Kent State University
Institute for Applied Linguistics
Address: 314 Satterfield Hall
Kent, OH 44242
Phone: (330) 672-1792
Website: http://appling.kent.edu/

Ohio State University
Slavic & East-European Languages & Literature
Address: Enarson Hall
154 W 12th Street
Columbus, OH 43210
Phone: (614) 292-6446
Website: http://www.osu.edu

Wright Sate University
Department of Modern Languages
Address: 133 Allyn Hall
3640 Colonel Glenn Highway
Dayton, OH 45435-0001
Phone: (937) 775-2641
Website: http://www.wright.edu

OKLAHOMA
Tulsa Community College
International Language Center
Address: 909 S Boston
Tulsa, OK 74119
Phone: (918) 595-7834
Website: http://www.tulsacc.edu

University of Central Oklahoma
Modern Languages, Literatures & Cultural Studies
Address: 100 North University Drive
Edmond, OK 73034
Phone: (405) 974-5647
Website: http://www.ucok.edu

PENNSYLVANIA
La Salle University
School of Arts & Sciences
Address: 1900 West Olney Avenue
Philadelphia, PA 19141
Phone: (215) 951-1100
Website: http://www.lasalle.edu

Pennsylvania State University
College of Liberal Arts
Address: 110 Sparks Building
University Park, PA 16802
Phone: (814) 865-7691
Website: http://www.psu.edu

PUERTO RICO
Universidad de Puerto Rico
Programa Graduado de Traduccion
Address: PO Box 22613
San Juan, PR 00931-2613
Phone: (809) 764-000 ext 2047
Website: http://www.upr.edu

SOUTH CAROLINA
College of Charleston
Mailing Address: 66 George Street
Charleston, SC 29424
Phone: (843) 805-5507
Website: http://www.cofc.edu

TENNESSEE
Tennessey Foreign Language Institute
Address: 227 French Landing
Suite 100
Nashville, TN 37228
Phone: (615) 741-7579
Website: http://ssreg.com/tfli

TEXAS
University of Texas at Arlington
Address: 701 S. Nedderman Drive
Arlington, TX 76019
Phone: (817) 272-2011
Website: http://www.uta.edu

University of Texas at Austin
Mailing Address: 1 University Station
Austin, TX 78712
Phone: 512) 475-7348
Website: http://www.utexas.edu

University of Texas at Dallas
Center for Translation Studies
Address: University of Texas at Dallas
Center for Translation Studies
P.O. Box 830688
Mail Station JO 51
Richardson, TX 75083-0688
Phone: (972) 883-2092
Website: www.utdallas.edu/

University of Texas at El Paso
Address: 500 West University Avenue
El Paso, TX 79968
Phone: (915) 747-5000
Website: http://www.utep.edu

UTAH
Brigham Young University
Department of Spanish & Portuguese
Address: 4050 JKHB
Provo, UT 84602
Phone: (801) 378-3465
Website: http://www.byu.edu

VIRGINIA
George Mason University
College of Education and Human Development
Address: George Mason University
4400 University Drive
Fairfax, VA 22030
Phone: (703) 993-1000
Website: www.gmu.edu/

James Madison University
Department of Foreign Languages, Literatures, and Cultures
Address: MSC 1802
James Madison University
Harrisonburg, VA 22807
Phone: (540) 568-6128
Website: www.jmu.edu/

WASHINGTON
American University
Department of Language and Foreign Studies
Address: The American University
Department of Language and Foreign Studies
Asbury Building – Room 324
4400 Massachussetts Avenue NW
Washington, DC 20016
Phone: (202) 885-3620
Website: www.american.edu/

Bellevue Community College
Translation and Interpretation Institute
Physical Address
BCC North Campus
10700 Northup, WA 98004
Mailing Address
3000 Landherholm Circle SE
Bellevue, WA 98007-6484
Phone: (425) 564-4000
Website: http://bellevuecollege.edu

University of Washington
Mailing Address (Admissions):
Schmitz Hall
Box 355852
Seattle, WA 98195-5852
Phone: (206) 543-2100
Website: http://www.washington.edu

Washington Academy of Languages
Translation & Interpretation Institute
Address: 98 Yesler Way
Seattle, WA 98104-2524
Phone: (206) 682-4463
Website: http://www.wal.org

WISCONSIN
University of Wisconsin
Graduate Certificate in Translation
Address: Graduate Certificate in Translation
UW-Milwaukee
Curtin Hall
P. O. Box 413
Milwaukee, WI 53201
Phone: (414) 229-1122 (General Information)
Website: www4.uwm.edu/

URUGUAY

Universidad de Montevideo
Facultad de Humanidades
Address: Universidad de Montevideo
Prudencio de Pena 2440
Montevideo – Uruguay
Phone: (598-2) 707 44 61
Website: www.um.edu.uy/

Universidad de la Republica
Facultad de Derecho
Main Address: Av. 18 de Julio 1968
Montevideo, Uruguay
Phone: (598-2) 4009201
Website: www.universidad.edu.uy/

VENEZUELA

Universidad Central de Venezuela
Facultad de Humanidades y Educación
Address: Universidad Central de Venezuela
Ciudad Universitaria
Los Chaguaramos
Caracas, Venezuela
Apartado Postal 1050
Phone: 58212-6054050
Website: www.ucv.ve/

GLOSSARY

Accreditation – Recognition granted by an entity to an organization, a program, an institution or a company to certify that they have met the predetermined standards and requirements of that entity.

American Translators Association (ATA) – Official organization of translators (and interpreters) located in the United States with members in over 90 countries.

Apostille – A separate document required by foreign countries pursuant to the Hague Convention of 1961 that authenticates a notarized document as a true copy of the original document. It also certifies the signature and seal of the notary. Apostilles are valid only in countries that participate in the Hague Convention of 1961. The Secretary of State in the United States is the entity that issues Apostilles. Note: An apostille does not certify that the content of a document is accurate.

ATA- See American Translators Association

Back Translation – The translation of a document that was already translated into a new language, and back to the original language. Usually, back translation is done to verify the accuracy of the translation.

CAT or C.A.T. Tools – See Computer Aided Translation Tools

CCR – See Central Contractor Registration

Central Contractor Registration (CCR) – This is the primary registrant database for the U.S. Federal Government.

Certification – 1) A Written statement attesting to the accuracy of a translation and the qualification of the translator, by the actual certified translator who performed the translation or by the translation company.

2) Recognition of professional competence granted by a recognized organization.

Certified Copy – The official copy (duplicate) of a document that has been notarized to attest that the copy is an exact and true copy of the original.

Certified Interpreter – A registered Court Interpreter who has passed the Court Interpreter Certification Examination and who is subject to abide by the Code of Professional Responsibility as established by the Court System. The requirements for Certified Interpreters vary in each State.

Certified Translation – A translated document that has been certified by a translation company or by a translator attesting to the fact that the translation was carried out by a qualified translator. Usually required for translation of official documents.

Computer Aided Translation Tools (CAT tools) – Computer program that allows a translator to work efficiently. A translation memory (TM) software is a type of CAT tool.

Conference Interpreter – A professional interpreter whose main task is to interpret simultaneously at conferences. At times, the interpreting is done consecutively, also. Conference Interpreting requires the use of microphones and earphones.

Consecutive Interpreting – Interpreting after the source language speaker has finished speaking. This type of interpreting usually allows the interpreter to take notes to assist in the interpretation.

Cultural Adaptation – Adapting a translation according to the cultural context of the target language (target audience).

Daily Output – The total (average) number of words a translator can translate on a daily basis.

Data Universal Numbering System (DUNS) – A unique nine digit number assigns by Dun & Bradstreet to a Company or Organization. This number is a universal number used to identify a Company or Organization and for keeping track of over 100 million businesses worldwide. It enables potential customers, suppliers, and lenders to easily identify and learn about a company.

Desktop Publishing – A graphic-oriented software program that allows a user to create high-quality materials for printing.

DUNS # - See Data Universal Numbering System

Editing – The process of thoroughly reviewing a translated document against the source document to ensure accuracy in translation; it involves making the necessary corrections, to reflect the accuracy in translation.

EIN – Employer Identification Number - An Employer Identification Number is a nine-digit number that is assigned by the IRS. The IRS uses the number to identify taxpayers that are required to file various business tax returns. EINs are used by employers, sole proprietors, corporations, partnerships, nonprofit associations, government agencies, certain individuals, and other business entities.

Employer Identification Number – See EIN above.

End-client – This is the "final" client for whom the translation is being done.

Errors and Omissions Insurance – This is an insurance policy that covers the insured (in this case the translator or translation company) against liability caused by errors or oversight made in the translation.

Escort Interpreting – This is when an interpreter accompanies a person, a group, or a delegation to their destination while interpreting for them.

File Transfer Protocol (FTP) – Common mean of sending files via the Internet and between computers. Often used to download or upload a file to a server.

Foreign Language – This is the language that is not spoken by the native people of a specific place or country.

Freelance (Freelancer) – An independent contractor who works on temporary projects for a set fee.

General Services Administration (GSA) – An independent agency of the United States government, established to help manage and support the basic functioning of federal agencies.

Globalization - 1) Term used to describe the process of creating, developing and adapting a good or service for distribution in various countries. 2) A company's business expansion into other countries.

GSA – See General Services Administration

GSA Schedule (General Services Administration Schedule) – A five-year contract with pre-negotiated prices, terms and conditions that allows commercial vendors to sell their products and/or services to the federal government. This contract has the potential to be renewed for 3 five-year periods.

HTML – See HyperText Markup Language

HyperText Markup Language (HTML) – A programming language with codes and symbols used in files to be used on the Web.

Interpretation – The rendering of oral conversation from one language into another.

Language Expansion – This occurs when the target language uses more words than the source language, or vice versa. Generally, the English language is compact. When translating from English into most Romance Languages (for example, French, Spanish, Italian, etc.) the word count is much greater in those languages than in the English language. The average **estimated** expansion for those languages is 25% (we must keep in mind, however, that style and subject area also influence the text expandability).

Localization – The process of customizing translation, usually software programs, to adapt to a specific international market or country.

Machine Translation (MT) – This is a translation performed by a computer.

MAS - See Multiple Award Schedule

Mistranslation – Incorrect or inaccurate translation.

MT – See Machine Translation

Multiple Award Schedule (MAS) – Also referred to as GSA Schedule and Federal Supply Schedule contracts, are indefinite delivery, indefinite quantity contracts available for use by federal agencies worldwide.

NAICS Code (North American Industry Classification System Code) – This is a standard code used by Federal statistical agencies in classifying business establishments for the purpose of collecting, analyzing and publishing statistical data related to U.S. business economy. The NAICS Code for the "Translation and Interpretation Services" sector is 541930.

NAJIT – See National Association of Judiciary Interpreters and Translators

National Association of Judiciary Interpreters and Translators (NAJIT) – A professional organization which seeks to promote quality interpretation and translation within the judicial system.

Native language – This is the first or primary language spoken by an individual.

Near-native speaker – A non-native speaker of a language who reaches a proficiency level that is equivalent to that of a native speaker of that language.

Net 30 (net 45) – This is a term of payment which specifies that payment is to be received 30 (45) days after the submission of the invoice.

Notarized Translation – Not to be confused with Certified Translation. A notary cannot attest to the validity of a certified translation. Usually, a notarized translation is one with a notarization authenticating the signature of the person who provided the certification of the translation.

OCR – See Optical Character Recognition

Omission - Omitting to translate a source word, source phrase, or any part from the source document.

Optical Character Recognition (OCR) – A software that converts pdf documents, scanned text and images into editable text files.

Oral Proficiency Interview (OPI) – This is a personal telephone interview administered in both English and a second language. The purpose of this interview is to evaluate the candidate's proficiency in the foreign language.

OPI – See Oral Proficiency Interview

PM – See Project Manager

Project Manager (PM) – Person responsible for overseeing and managing translation projects in all of their phases; this includes receiving the projects from the clients, assigning the translation projects to the appropriate translators, editors and proofreaders, and at times to the appropriate desktop publisher (in-house or freelance), handling cost management, overseeing quality control and timely delivery.

Proofreading – A thorough review of a translated document to ensure there are no formatting errors, no typographical errors, no incorrect grammar, no punctuation or spelling errors. In translation, the proofreader does not have to work with the source document to perform the proofreading.

Purchase Order (PO) – A written authorization prepared by a Company (Translation Company) with complete details of the services to be rendered, the time of delivery, along with the project reference or job number and price and issued to the service provider.

Quality Control (QC) – A system of verifying output in order to ensure that the high quality requirements and standards have been met.

Registered Interpreter – An interpreter who is registered by the Court after having passed a Language Fluency Examination. The requirements for registered interpreters vary in each State.

Request for Quotation or Request for Quote (RFQ) – This is a document used by an organization to request bids from suppliers of products or services. An RFQ is a more rigid-type of request, with little or no room for change in price, as it is oriented toward a fixed project or service.

Request for Proposal (RFP) – A document prepared by a company or institution requesting to receive bids from potential vendors/providers of products or services. An RFP is a more flexible-type of request, where the proposed price may change according to changes in parameters.

RFP – See Request for Proposal

RFQ – See Request for Quotation

Sight Translation – Oral or written "translation" of a written text without prior preparation.

Sign Language – Language of gestures and facial expressions used as a means of communication.

Simultaneous Interpreting – Interpreting as the source language speaker is still speaking.

Source language - The language in which the original text to be translated is written.

Source word – Word found in the original or source document that is to be translated.

Subcontractor – An individual or company hired by a general or main contractor to perform a specific service.

Target Audience – This is the intended audience, party or market for whom a translation is being done.

Target language – The language into which the original text will be translated.

Target word – Word found in the translated document.

Telephone Interpreting – Interpreting of telephonic conversations.

Terminology Management – A method of identifying and compiling terms, creating a glossary with those terms and maintaining and using the glossary efficiently.

TM – See Translation Memory

Track Change Mode – A feature in MS Word that allows for one or more users to edit a document using different font colors. The final reviewer has the option of accepting or rejecting the insertions and/or deletions, which will then be incorporated into the final document.

Transcription – The process of converting spoken language into written text.

Translation – This is the process of rendering written text from one language into another language while taking into account the context, grammatical rules and cultural adaptation.

Translation Memory (TM) – This is a database which stores sentences and their translations for use in future translations.

Transliteration – A process of converting characters (letters or words) in one alphabet or phonetic sounds into another alphabet.

Vendor – One who sells services (or products).

Voice-Over (VO)- The audio recording of translated text to be used on video or audio media.

ABC TRANSLATIONS, INC.
1122 Adam Street; Anywhere, USA 11111
Ph: (123) 245-6789; Fax: (123) 888-4555
www.abctranslations.com
info@abctranslations.com

PURCHASE ORDER

Date : Monday, January 1, 2008   **PO # :** 365902

Vendor: Mary Smith

Email: msmith@aol.com   **Phone No. :** (123)-456-7890

PROJECT INFORMATION

Job No. 82653   **Project Manager :** Victoria Allen
Project Description : Translation of 12 Medical Consent Forms
Source Language : English   **Target Language :** Spanish
Word Count : 16,874   **Payment :** $0.12/source word

Please Note :
Our payment terms are Net 30 days from receipt of your invoice. Include the Project Number, Project Manager's name, and Description of Services for faster processing. Invoice processing will begin when we receive your e-mailed or faxed invoice addressed to info@abctranslations.com.

Delivery Date: **01/16/2008 by 9:00A.M.**
Delivery Method: Email

SPECIAL INSTRUCTIONS: Translation to be submitted in Word Format.
Please send all translations to VAllen@abctranslations.com

*Do not start a job until you have received a purchase order and have verified that all the information on this Purchase Order is correct. If you find a discrepancy, contact the Project Manager before beginning any work, and you will receive a revised Purchase Order. If you are not able to meet the requested deadline, please contact your Project Manager immediately.

Please confirm receipt of this Order.

INVOICE

MARY SMITH
SSN: 450-34-1234
msmith@aol.com

Address: 123 ABC Avenue
Anywhere, USA 12345
Phone: (123) 456-7890
Fax: (123) 456-7980

Invoice Date: January 16, 2008

Scheduled Completion Date: January 16, 2008

Job #:   82653

PO #:   365902

Project Manager: Victoria Allen

Job Description: Translation of 12 Medical Consent Forms from English into Spanish

Delivery Format: Word file via e-mail

Billed To: **ABC Translations, Inc.**

1122 Adam Street

Anywhere, USA 11111

Please pay this amount: **$2,024.88**

Make Check Payable to **Mary Smith** and mail to above address.

I thank you for your continued business!!!

APPENDIX C
SAMPLE TRANSLATOR RESUME

MARY SMITH
PROFESSIONAL TRANSLATOR
123 ABC AVENUE
Anywhere, USA 12345

Phone: (123) 456-7890
Fax: (123) 456-7980
Mobile: (123) 678-4455
Email: msmith@aol.com

OBJECTIVE: Seeking to provide translation, editing and proofreading services from French into English and English into Spanish on a freelance basis.

QUALIFICATIONS

B.A. in Modern Languages from University of Florida
Certificate in General Translation from New York University
Native Speaker of English; Near-native Spanish speaker; Fluent in French
Have over 5 years experience in field of Translation

EQUIPMENT & SOFTWARE

IBM compatible Intel Pentium 4 CPU; Laser Printer; Fax
High speed internet connection; Windows XP, Microsoft Office XP Professional
Adobe Acrobat 8 Professional, SDL Trados 2007 ; Many USB Flash Drives 1 GB capacity (Each); Energizer Power Protection/Home Battery Backup 650 VA

RELEVANT INFORMATION

<u>Areas of expertise:</u> Medical, pharmaceutical, commercial, business, financial, legal, academia, general.

MARY SMITH (CONTINUED)

Equipped with various monolingual and bilingual dictionaries [French <>English; Spanish<>English; general and specialized], reference manuals, grammar and stylistic books in English, French and Spanish.

Type: 60WPM; Average Daily Output: 2000 words

PROFESSIONAL AFFILIATIONS

Member of the American Translators Association (ATA)

TRANSLATION/EDITING/PROOFREADING EXPERIENCE

- Recently translated from French into English, a 50,000 words children's book (5-month project)
- Translated from English into Spanish various labor manuals, social services documents and various academic documents for middle school children
- Edited and proofread from French into English legal and commercial documents, pharmaceutical and health-related documents

ADDITIONAL INFORMATION:

10/05-01/06 Worked as a volunteer Interpreter of Spanish and English for the American Red Cross

11/06- Present Translate immigration documents from French into English on a pro-bono basis for a charitable organization

REFERENCES: Available upon request

Sample 1

MARY SMITH
Professional Translator & Editor
English> Spanish and French>English

Phone #:   (123) 456-7890   123 ABC Avenue
Fax #:   (123) 456-7980   Anywhere, USA 12345
msmith@aol.com

Sample 2

MARY SMITH
Certified Translator
Professional Editor & Proofreader
English> Spanish and French> English

Phone #:   (123) 456-7890   123 ABC Avenue
Fax #:   (123) 456-7980   Anywhere, USA 12345
msmith@aol.com

Endnotes

1. http://en.wikipedia.org/wiki/Translation
3. http://www.septuagint.net/
4. http://www.notablebiographies.com/Ch-Co/Chaucer-Geoffrey.html
5. http://faculty.smu.edu/bwheeler/Ency/ktale.html
6. http://search.eb.com/shakespeare/article-754
A. Bureau of Labor Statistics, U.S. Department of Labor, Occupational Outlook Handbook, 2008-09 Edition, Interpreters and Translators; http://www.bls.gov/oco/ocos175.htm
B. Federal Register/ Volume 65, No. 159, Wednesday, August 16, 2000 / Notices

Sources

Orbach, S. & Nelson, J. **Getting a GSA Schedule,** ISBN 1-4196-3264-7

The ATA Chronicle, November/December 2007, Volume XXXVI, Number 11, Page 38 "Business Smart – Liability Clauses"

The ATA Chronicle, October 2007, Volume XXXVI, Number 10, Page 18, "Insult to Injury: When Your Client Goes Bankrupt" by Mike Collins

Abyy Finereader, Optical Character Recognition (OCR) Software; http://www.abbyy.com

Accounting Software Advisor; http://www.accountingsoftwareadvisor.com

Accounting Software Review; http://accounting-software-review.toptenreviews.com

Accounting Software, (Quicken, Quickbooks, TurboTax, etc); http://www.intuit.com

Acronym Finder Online; http://www.acronymfinder.com

Adobe Dreamweaver, Website Creation Software; http://www.adobe.com

Amazon.ca; Canada; http://www.amazon.ca

Amazon.com. U.S.A.; http://www.amazon.com

Amazon.fr; France; http://www.amazon.fr

American Translators Association (ATA), ATA News and Activities, ATA Members and Internet Scams Update; http://www.atanet.org/ata_activities/internet_scams.php

AnyCount, Word Count Software; http://www.anycount.com

Argos Translations, http://www.argostranslations.com

Barnes and Noble, Online; http://www.barnesandnoble.com

Blackwell Bookshop Online; http://www.bookshop.blackwell.co.uk

Books-A-Million Online Bookstore; http://www.booksamillion.com

Borders, Online; http://www.borders.com

Bureau of Labor Statistics, U.S. Department of Labor, Occupational Outlook Handbook, 2008-09 Edition, Interpreters and Translators; http://www.bls.gov/oco/ocos175.htm

CanTalk Canada, http://www.cantalk.com

Central Contractor Registration; http://www.ccr.gov

Central Intelligence Agency (CIA), Employment Opportunities; http://www.cia.gov/careers

Collection Agency Research, Online Resource for Information on Debt Collection Agency; http://www.collectionagencyresearch.com

Cyracom, http://www.cyracom.com

Déja Vu, Translation Memory Software; http://www.atril.com

Department of Defense (DoD), Employment Opportunities; http://www.defenselink.mil/

Dictionary Online; http://www.alphadictionary.com

Dun & Bradstreet, Company Profile Report: Eriksen Translations, Inc. (Report as of March 12, 2008), https://smallbusiness.dnb.com/

Dun & Bradstreet; http://www.dnb.com

DUNS Number, About DUNS Number; http://www.dnb.com/US/duns_update

EducaVision; http://www.educavision.com

Efax, Electronic Faxing; http://www.efax.com

Etranslate, http://www.etranslate.com

ExactSpent, Time Tracking Software; http://www.exactspent.com

EZGSA; http://www.EZGSA.com

Federal Bureau of Investigations (FBI), Employment Opportunities; http://www.fbijobs.gov

Federeal Business Opportunities; http://www.fedbizopps.gov

Find Accounting Software; www.findaccountingsoftware.com

FIT-Europe, Information on how to claim debt from Bad Payers in countries outside Europe; http://www.fit-europe.org/ (Projects, Bad Payers, Material Already Received)

French and European Publications Inc.; http://www.frencheuropean.com

Google, General Searches; http://www.google.com

Harvard Bookstore; http://www.harvard.com

International Monetary Fund (IMF), International Organization; http://www.imf.org (About the IMF)

Internet Crime Complaint Center (IC3) ; http://www.ic3.gov

InTrans Book Service; http://www.intransbooks.com

La Maison du dictionnaire; http://www.dicoland.com

Librairie Eyrolles; http://www.eyrolles.com

Librairie Michel Fortin; http://www.librairiemichelfortin.com

Libreri Mapou; http://www.librerimapou.com

Lionbridge, Corporate News, http://www.lionbridge.com

Microsoft FrontPage, Website Creation Software; http://www.microsoftfrontpage.com

Microsoft Office Accounting Express 2008; http://www.office.microsoft.com

Microsoft Word, Word Count Feature; http://office.microsoft.com/en-us/word/HA012303581033.aspx#3

Moneybookers.com, Payment Methods; http://www.moneybookers.com (About Us page)

MYOB Premier Accounting 2008; http://www.myob.com

National Association of Small Business Contractors; http://www.nasbc.org

National Consumers League's Internet Fraud Watch; http://fraud.org/tips/internet/fakecheck.htm

National Virtual Translation Center (NVTC); http://www.nvtc.gov

Nova Information Systems (currently Elavon), Merchant Account Services; http://www.novainfo.com

Omnipage, Optical Character Recognition (OCR) Software; http://www.nuance.com (Products)

Oxford University Press; http://www.oup.co.uk

Payment Practices, Payment Issues and Collection Agencies; http://www.paymentpractices.net

PayPal, Payment Methods; http://www.paypal.com (About Us page)

Peachtree Complete Accounting; http://www.peachtree.com

Peachtree Quantum; http://www.peachtreequantum.com

Pierre Books; http://www.pierrebooks.com

Planet Translation, Universities Offering Programs in Translation and/or Interpretation; http://planettranslation.com/career-univ.html

Powell's Books, Online; http://www.powells.com

PractiCount & Invoice, Word Count and Line Count Software; http://www.
practiline.com
Proz.com, Blue Board, Database with Information about Translation
Companies and their
Payment Methods; http://www.proz.com/blueboard
Proz.com, Online Networking Venues; http://www.proz.com
R.M.S., Payment Issues and Collection Agencies; http://www.rmsna.com
(About Us page)
Renaud-Bray; http://www.renaud-bray.com
Sage Software; http://www.sagesoftware.com
Schreiber Publishing, Inc.; http://www.schreiberpublishing.com
SDL Trados 2007, Translation Memory Software; http://www.translationzone.
com
Simply Accounting Entrepreneur; http://www.simplyaccounting.com
Site Spinner, Website Creation Software; http://www.virtualmechanics.com
Testing and Certification Program (LTC); www1.dshs.wa.gov/msa/ltc
The American Book Center; http://www.abc.nl
The National Association of Judiciary Interpreters and Translators, NAJIT,
About NAJIT; http://www.najit.org
The North Atlantic Treaty Organization (NATO), International Organization;
http://www.nato.int
The United Nations, About the United Nations; http://www.un.org
The United Nations, Examinations and Tests Section, Language Proficiency
Examinations (LPE); http://www.un.org/exam/lpe
The World Bank, International Organization; www.worldbank.org
Translation and Interpretation Schools; http://www.proz.com/translators_
associations
Translation and Interpreting Schools, American Translators Association ,
Certification, List of Approved Translation and Interpreting Schools;
http://www.atanet.org/certification/eligibility_approved.php
Translation Memory, Definition; http://en.wikipedia.org/wiki/Translation_
memory
Translation Office 3000; http://www.to3000.com
Translators' Associations, Proz.com; http://www.proz.com/translators_
associations

TranslatorsBase.com, Online Networking Venues; http://www.translatorsbase.com

TranslatorsCafé.com, Online Networking Venues; http://www.translatorscafe.com

Transperfect, http://www.transperfect.com

TTIs Brazil; http://isg.urv.es/tti/brazil.html

TTIs Italy; www.isg.urv.es/tti/italy.html

TTIs Japan; http://isg.urv.es/tti/japan.html

U.S. Census Bureau, North American Industry Classification System, NAICS; http://www.census.gov/eos/www/naics/

U.S. Courts, Bankruptcy Laws; http://www.uscourts.gov/bankruptcycourts/bankruptcybasics.html

U.S. Department of State; http://www.state.gov

U.S. General Services Administration, Definition; http://en.wikipedia.org/wiki/General_Services_Administration

U.S. General Services Administration; http://www.gsa.gov

U.S. Small Business Administration; http://www.sba.gov

USA JOBS, U.S. Government Employment Opportunities; http://www.usajobs.com

VistaPrint, Online Printing Services; http://www.vistaprint.com

Washington State Department of Social and Health Services, DSHS, About DSHS; www1.dshs.wa.gov

Washington State Department of Social and Health Services, DSHS, The Language

Web Easy Professional, Website Creation Software; http://www.webeasyprofessional.com

Web Page Maker, Website Creation Software; http://www.webpage-maker.com

Web Plus, Website Creation Software; http://www.serif.com

Web Studio, Website Creation Software; http://www.webstudio.com

Word Reference Online; http://www.wordreference.com

Wordfast, Translation Memory Software; http://www.wordfast.net

World Health Organization (WHO), International Organization; http://www.who.int (About WHO)

Xoom, Payment Methods, Money Transfers; http://www.xoom.com

ACE Traductores (ACEtt); http://www.acett.org
American Literary Translators Association (ALTA); http://www.utdallas.edu/alta
American Translators Association (ATA); http://www.atanet.org
Arabic Translation and Intercultural Dialogue (ATIDA); http://www.atida.org
Asociación Aragonesa de Traductores e Intérpretes (ASATI); http://www.asati.es
Asociación Argentina de Traductores e Intérpretes (AATI); http://www.aati.org.ar/
Asociación Colombiana de Traductores e Intérpretes (ACTI); http://www.traductorescolombia.com
Asociación de Intérpretes de Conferencias de la Argentina (ADICA); http://www.adica.org.ar/
Asociación de Traductores e Intérpretes de Monterrey (ATIMAC); http://www.atimac.org.mx/
Asociación de Traductores e Intérpretes del Ecuador (ATIEC); http://www.atiec.org
Asociación de Traductores Profesionales del Perú (ATPP); http://www.atpp.org/esp
Asociación Galega de Profesionais da Traducción e da Interpretación (AGPTI); http://www.agpti.org/castelan/
Asociación Guatemalteca de Intérpretes y Traductores (AGIT); http://www.agitguatemala.org
Asociación Profesional Española de Traductores e Intérpretes (APETI); http://www.apeti.org.es/
Associação Brasileira de Tradutores (ABRATES); http://www.abrates.com.br/
Associação Portuguesa de Tradutores (APT); http://www.apt.pt/
Association des Traducteurs et Interprètes de L'Ontario/
Association of Translators and Interpreters of Ontario (ATIO); http://www.atio.on.ca/
Association des Traducteurs Littéraires de France (ATLF); http://www.atlf.org
Association of Finnish Translation Companies (SKTOL); http://www.sktol.org
Association of Translation Companies (ATC); http://www.atc.org.uk
Association of Translators and Interpreters of Alberta (ATIA); http://www.atia.ab.ca/

Association of Translators and Interpreters of Manitoba (ATIM)/ Association des traducteurs et interprètes du Manitoba http:// www.atim. mb.ca/

Association of Translators and Interpreters of Nova Scotia (ATINS); http:// www.atins.org

Association Professionnelle des Métiers de la Traduction (APROTRAD); http://www.aprotrad.org

Association Suisse des Traducteurs Jurés (ASTJ); http://www.astj.ch/

Association Suisse des Traducteurs, Terminologues et Interprètes (ASTTI); http://www.astti.ch/

Associazione Italiana Traduttori e Interpreti (AITI); http://www.aiti.org

Associazione Nazionale Interpreti di Conferenza Professionisti (ASSOINTERPRETI); http://www.assointerpreti.it

Associazione Nazionale Italiana Traduttori e Interpreti (ANITI); http://www. aniti.it

Atlanta Association of Interpreters and Translators (AAIT); http://www.aait.org

Australian Institute of Interpreters and Translators (AUSIT); http://www. ausit.org

Austrian Association of Certified Court Interpreters (AACI); http://www. gerichtsdolmetscher.at/

Belgian Chamber of Translators, Interpreters and Philologists/(Chambre belge des traducteurs, interprètes et philologues / Belgische Kamer van Vertalers, Tolken en Filologen [CBTIP/BKVTF]); http://www.cbtip-bkvtf.org

Carolina Association of Translators and Interpreters (CATI); http://www. catiweb.org

Chartered Institute of Linguists (IOL); http://www.iol.org.uk/

Colegio de Traductores del Perú (CTP); http://www.colegiodetraductores. org.pe/

Colegio de Traductores e Intérpretes de Chile (COTICH); http://www. traductores-agts.cl/

Colegio de Traductores Públicos del Uruguay (CTPU); http://www. colegiotraductores.org.uy/

Delaware Valley Translators Association (DVTA); http://www.dvta.org

European Society for Translation Studies (EST); http://www.est-translationstudies.org

Fédération Internationale des Traducteurs (FIT) / International Federation of Translators; http://www.fit-ift.org

Hellenic Association of Translators & Interpreters (HATI); http://www.hati.org.uk/

Honk Kong Translation Society; http://www.hkts.org.hk/

Indian Translators Association (ITAINDIA); http://www.itaindia.org

Japan Association of Translators (JAT); http://www.jat.org

Japan Translation Federation Incorporated (JTF); http://www.jft.jp/

Literary Translators' Association of Canada (LTAC) / Association des Traducteurs et Traductrices Littéraires du Canada; http://www.attlc-ltac.org

Localization Industry Standards Association (LISA); http://www.lisa.org

Michigan Translators/Interpreters Network (MiTiN); http://www.mitinweb.org

Mid-America Chapter of ATA (MICATA); http://www.ata-micata.org

Midwest Association of Translators and Interpreters (MATI); http://www.matiata.org

National Accreditation Authority for Translators and Interpreters (NAATI); http://www.naati.org.au/

National Capital Area Chapter of ATA (NCATA); http://www.ncata.org

New York Circle of Translators (NYCT); http://www.nyctranslators.org

Northeast Ohio Translators Association (NOTA); http://www.notatranslators.org

Northern California Translators Association (NCTA); http://www.ncta.org

Northwest Translators and Interpreters Society (NOTIS); http://www.notisnet.org

Organización Mexicana de Traductores (OMT); http://www.omt.org.mx/

Panhellenic Association of Professional Translators (PAPT); http://www.psem.gr/

Sindicato Nacional dos Tradutores (SINTRA); http://www.sintra.org.br/

Société Française des Traducteurs (SFT); http://www.sft.fr

Society of Translators and Interpreters of British Columbia (S.T.I.B.C.); http://www.stibc.org

Taiwan Association of Translation and Interpretation (TATI); http://www.tati.org.tw/

The American Association of Language Specialists (TAALS); http://www.taals.net

The California Court Interpreter Association (CCIA); http://www.ccia.org

The Institute of Translation and Interpreting (ITI); http://www.iti.org.uk

The Translators' Association (TTA); http://www.societyofauthors.org/subsidiary_groups/translators_association

Translators Association of China; http://www.tac-online.org.cn

Ukrainian Translators' Association (UTA); http://www.uta.org.ua

Upper Midwest Translators and Interpreters Association (UMTIA); http://www.umtia.com

Washington State Court Interpreters and Translators Society (WITS); http://www.witsnet.org

----

Aarhus School of Administration; http://www.asb.dk/

Akademia Polonisjna w Częstochowie/Polonia University in Czestochowa; http://www.ap.edu.pl/

Al-Alsun University; http://www.als.shams.edu.eg/

Alianza Francesa de Cuba; http://es/afcuba.org/

Al-Mustansiriyah University; http://www.uomustansiriyah.edu.iq/

American University; http://www.american.edu/

Arizona State University; http://www.asu.edu/tempe/

Aston University; http://www1.aston.ac.uk/

Auckland Institute of Technology; http://www.aut.ac.nz/

Babes-Bolyai University/Universtatea BABEŞ-BOLYAI; http://www.ubbcluj.ro/

Bangalore University; http://www.bub.ernet.in/

Bar-Ilan University; http://www1.biu.ac.il/

Beijing Foreign Studies University (Bei Wai); http://www.bfsu.edu.cn

Beijing International Studies University (BISU); http://www.bisu.edu.cn/

Bellevue Community College; http://bellevuecollege.edu

Bilkent University; http://www.bilkent.edu.tr/

Binghamton University; http://trip@binghamton.edu

Bogaziçi University; http://www/boun.edu.tr/

Boston University Center for Professional Education; http://www.umasstranslation.com

Brigham Young University; http://www.byu.edu
Brooklyn College; http://www.brooklyn.cuny.edu
Burapha University; http://www.buu.ac.th/
California State University; http://www.calstate.edu
Caritas Francis Hsu College; http://www.cfhc.caritas.edu.hk/
Centre for English Language and Training; http://www.celt.edu.gr/
Centro Universitario Iberoamericano (UNIBERO); http://www.ibero.br/
Charles University; http://www.cuni.cz
Chinese University of Hong Kong (CUHK); http://www.cuhk.edu.hk/
Chulalongkorn University; http://www.chula.ac.th/
City University of Hong Kong; http://www.cityu.edu.hk/
College of Charleston; http://www.cofc.edu
Cologne University of Applied Sciences /Fachhochschule Köln; http://www.
    fh-koeln.de/
Columbia University; http://www.barnard.columbia.edu
Comenius University; http://www.univa.sk/
Concordia University; http://www.concordia.ca
Corporación Universitaria de Colombia Ideas; http://www.ideas.edu.co/
Daito Bunka University; http://www2.daito.ac.jp/en/
Deakin University; http://www.deakin.edu.au
Dublin City University (DCU); http://www.dcu.ie/
Ecole Superieure de Traducteurs et d'Interpretes (ESIT); http://www.esit.
    univ-paris3.fr
École Supérieure Roi Fahd de Traduction; http://www.ecoleroifahd.uae.ma/
Edith Cowan University; http://www.ecu.edu.au
Eötvös Loránd University (ELTE); http://www.elte.hu/
Erasmushogeschool; http://www.ehb.be
Escola Superior de Tecnologia e Gestão do Instituto Politécnico de Leiria;
    http://www.estg.ipleiria.pt
Escuela Americana de Traductores e Intérpretes (EATRI); http://www.eatri.cl
Escuela Profesional de Traducción e Interpretación; http://www.epti-
    translation.com
Florida A&M University; http://www.famu.edu
Florida International University; http://w3.fiu.edu/translation/
Fu Jen Catholic University; http://www.fju.edu.tw/
George Mason University; http://www.gmu.edu/

202

Georgia State University; http://www.gsu.edu/
Hacettepe University; http://www.hacettepe.edu.tr/
Hankuk University of Foreign Studies; http://www.hufs.ac.kr/user/
hufsenglish/
Hochschule Magdeburg – Stendal (FH)/University of Applied Sciences;
http://www.fachkommunikation.hs-magdeburg.de
Hogeschool West-Nederland; http://www.west-nederland.nl/
Humboldt Universität zu Berlin; http://www.hu-berlin.de/
Hunter College; http://www.hunter.cuny.edu
Indiana University; http://www.indiana.edu
Institut Cooremans; http://www.brunette.brucity.be/ferrer/cooremans/index.
html
Institut Libre Marie Haps; http://www.ilmh.be
Institut Supérieur de Traducteurs et Interprètes; http://www.heb.be/isti
Institut Superieur d'Interpretariat et de Traduction (ISIT); http://www.isit-
paris.fr
Instituto Nacional de Educación Superior No. 28 "Olga Cossettini," Rosario;
http://www.iesoc.com.ar
Instituto Profesional ELADI; http://http://eladi.cl/
Instituto Superior de Assistentes e Intérpretes; http://isg.urv.es/tti/portugal.
html
Instituto Superior de Interpretes y Traductores; http://www.isit.edu.mx/
Inter School; http://www.interschool.jp/
International Christian University; http://www.icu.ac.jp/
Istanbul University; http://www.istanbul.edu.tr/
Istituto Superiore Interpreti Traduttori (ISIT); http://www.scuolecivichemilano.
it/
Istituto Superiore per Interpreti e Traduttori (ISIT); http://www.
ssmlmaddaloni.it/
James Madison University; http://www.jmu.edu/
Johannes Gutenberg-Universität Mainz in Germersheim; http://www.uni-
mainz.de/
Karazin Kharkiv National University; http://www.univer.kharkov.ua/
Kent State University; http://appling.kent.edu/
King Saud University; http://www.ksu.edu.sa/

Kyoto Tachibana Women's University; http://www.tashibama-u.ac/jp/
english
La Salle University; http://www.lasalle.edu
Lingnan University; http://www.LN.edu.hk/
Linguistic University of Nizhny Novgorod; http://www.dia.lunn.ru/
Macquarie University; http://www.mq.au
Martin-Luther-Universität Halle-Wittenberg; http://www.uni-halle.de/
Marygrove College; http://www.marygrove.edu
Marymount Manhattan College; http://www.mmm.edu
McGill University; http://www.mcgill.ca
Metafrasi School of Translation Studies; http://www.metafrasi.edu.gr/
Miami Dade College; http://www.mdc.edu/
Middlesex University; http://www.mdx.ac.uk/
Montclair State University; http://www.montclair.edu
Monterrey Institute of International Studies; http://translate.miis.edu/
National Hispanic University; http://www.nhu.edu
National Taiwan Normal University (NTNU); http://www.ntnu.edu.tw/
National University; http:///www.nu.edu/
New York University, School of Continuing and Professional Studies; http://
www.scps.nyu.edu/
Newcastle University; http://www.ncl.ac.uk/
Northern Illinois University; http://www.niu.edu/
Notre Dame University; http://www.ndu.edu.lb/
Oakland University; http://www2.oakland.edu
Ohio State University; http://www.osu.edu
Osaka University of Foreign Studies; http://www.osaka-u.ac.jp/eng/
Pennsylvania State University; http://www.psu.edu
Perm State University; http://www.psu.ru/
Pima Community College; http://www.pima.edu
Politécnico Colombo Andino; http://www.polcolan.edu.co/
Pontificia Universidad Católica Argentina Santa María de los Buenos Aires;
http://www.uca.edu.ar
Pontificia Universidad Católica de Chile; http://www.uc.cl/
Pontifícia Universidade Católica de Rio de Janeiro (PUC-RIO); http://www.
puc-rio.br/
Pontifícia Universidade Católica de São Paulo (PUC-SP); http://www.pucsp.br/

Queens College; http://www.qc.cuny.edu

Queen's University; http://www.queensu.ca

Ramkhamhaeng University; http://www.ru.ac.th/

Rose-Hulman Institute of Technology; http://www.rose-hulman.edu/

Royal Melbourne Institute of Technology; http:www.rmit.edu.au

Rutgers University; http://www.rutgers.edu

San Diego State University; http://www.sdsu.edu/

Shanghai International Studies University; http://giit.shisu.edu.cn

Southbank Institute of Technology; http://www.southbank.edu.au

Southern California School of Interpretation; http://www.interpreting.com/

SSML Gregorio VII; http://www.gregoriosettimo.eu

St. Olaf College; http://www.stolaf.edu

St. Petersburg State University; http://www.www.spbu.ru/e/

Stanford University; http://www.stanford.edu

Stockholm University / Stockholms Universitet; http://www.su.se/

Tennessey Foreign Language Institute; http://ssreg.com/tfli

Thammasat University; http://www.tu.ac.th/

The American University; http://www.aucegypt.edu/

The Copenhagen Business School; http://uk.cbs.dk/

The Ionian University; http://www.ionio.gr/

The University of Auckland; http://www.auckland.ac.nz/

The University of Hong Kong; http://www.hku.hk/

Toyo Eiwa Women's University; http://www.toyoeiwa.ac.jp/

Tulsa Community College; http://www.tulsacc.edu

Universidad Adventista del Plata; http://www.uapar.edu

Universidad Alfonso X el Sabio; http://www.uax.es/

Universidad Autonoma de Baja California; http://www.uabc.mx/

Universidad Autónoma de Manizales; http://www.autonoma.edu.co/

Universidad Autónoma de Tlaxcala; http://www.uatx.mx/

Universidad Católica de Valparaíso; http:www.pucv.cl/

Universidad Central de Venezuela; http://www.ucv.ve/

Universidad de Alicante; http://www.uab.es/

Universidad de Belgrano; http://www.ub.edu.ar

Universidad de Buenos Aires; http://www.uba.ar

Universidad de Castilla-La Mancha; http://www.uclm.es/

Universidad de Granada; http://www.ugr.es/

Universidad de la Republica; http://www.universidad.edu.uy/
Universidad de Las Palmas de Gran Canaria; http://www.ulpgc.es/
Universidad de Málaga; http://www.uma.es/
Universidad de Montevideo; http://www.um.edu.uy/
Universidad de Morón; http://www.unimoron.edu.ar
Universidad de Puerto Rico; http://www.upr.edu
Universidad de Salamanca; http://exlibris.usal.es/
Universidad del Salvador; http://www.salvador.edu.ar
Universidad Femenina del Sagrado Corazón (UNIFE); http://www.unife.
    edu.pe/
Universidad Intercontinental; http://www.uic.edu.mx/
Universidad Nacional de Catamarca; http://www.unca.edu.ar
Universidad Nacional de Colombia (CUTRA); www.unal.edu.co/
Universidad Nacional de Córdoba; http://www.unc.edu.ar
Universidad Nacional de La Plata; http://www.unlp.edu.ar
Universidad Pontificia Comillas; http://www.upcomillas.es/
Universidad Ricardo Palma/Ricardo Palma University; http://www.urp.edu.pe/
Universidad Santiago de Cali; http://www.usc.edu.co/
Universidade Autónoma de Lisboa; http://www.universidade-autonoma.pt/
Universidade Castelo Branco (UCB); http://www.castelobranco.br/
Universidade Cidade de São Paulo (UNICID); http://www.unicid.br/
Universidade de Coimbra; http://uc.pt/
Universidade de Lisboa; http://www.ul.pt/
Universidade de São Paulo. Centro Interdepartamental de Tradução e
    Terminologia (USP-CITRAT); http://www.fflch.usp.br/citrat/citrat.
    htm
Universidade de Vigo; http://www.webs.uvigo.es/
Universidade do Minho; http://www.uminho.pt/
Universidade do Porto; http://www.up.pt/
Universidade Estadual de Campinas (UNICAMP); http://www.unicamp.br/
Universidade Federal de Juiz de For a; http://www.ufjf.br/
Universidade Federal Fluminense; http://www.uff.br/
Universidade Mackenzie; http://www.mackenzie.br/
Università degli Studi di Trieste; http://www.sslmit.univ.trieste.it/
Università di Bologna; http://www.ssit.unibo.it/
Università di Lecce; http://www.lingue.unile.it/

Universität Bonn; http://www1.uni-bonn.de/
Universität Graz; http://www.kfunigraz.ac.at/
Universität Innsbruck; http://www.uibk.ac.at/
Universitat Pompeu Fabra; http://www.upf.edu/factii/
Université Charles de Gaulle – Lille 3; http://www.univ-lille3.fr/
Université d'Alger; http://www.univ-alger.dz
Université d'Orléans; http://www.univ-orleans.fr/lettres
Université de Haute-Alsace; http://www.fsesj.uha.fr/
Université de Moncton; http://www.umoncton.ca
Universitè de Mons-Hainaut; http://www.umh.ac.be
Université de Montréal; http://www.umontreal.com
Université de Nice - Sophia Antipolis; http://lettres.unice.fr/
Université de Pau et des Pays de l'Adour (UPPA); http://www.univ-pau.fr
Université de Saint-Esprit de Kaslik (USEK)/Holy Spirit University; http://
    www.usek.edu.lb/
Université de Toulouse II- Le Mirail; http://w3.univ-tlse2.fr/
Université du Québec; http://www.uquebec.ca
Université Laval; http://www.lli.ulaval.ca
Université Marc Bloch; http://www.itiri.com
Université Saint-Joseph; http://www.usj.edu.lb/
Université Sorbonne Nouvelle – Paris 3; http://www.univ-paris3.fr/
Universiteit Utrecht/ Utrecht University; http://www.uu.nl/
Universiteit van Amsterdam/University of Amsterdam; http://www.uva.nl/
Universitetet I Agder/Agder University; http://www.uia.no/en
University of Arizona; http://ncitrp.web.arizona.edu/
University of Arkansas; http://www.uark.edu/
University of Birmingham; http://www.cels.bham.ac.uk/
University of British Columbia; http://www.ubc.ca
University of California; www.uclaextension.edu/
University of Central Oklahoma; http://www.ucok.edu
University of Copenhagen; http://www.ku.dk/
University of Debrecen; http://www.unideb.hu/
University of Denver; http://www.universitycollege.du.edu
University of Florida; http://www.ufl.edu/
University of Geneva / Université de Genève; www.unige.ch/
University of Hawaii at Manoa; http://www.uhm.hawaii.edu/

University of Helsinki; http://www.helsinki.fi/university/
University of Hyderabad; http://www.uohyd.ernet.in/
University of Illinois at Urbana Champaign; http://www.uiuc.edu
University of Indonesia; http://www.ui.edu
University of Iowa; http://www.uiowa.edu
University of Joensuu; http://www.joensuu.fi
University of Johannesburg; http://www.uj.ac.za/
University of Jordan; http://www.ju.edu.jo/
University of Latvia; http://www.lu.lv/eng/
University of Leeds; http://www.leeds.ac.uk/
University of Maryland; http://www.umd.edu/
University of Nebraska; http://www.nebraska.edu/
University of New England; http://www.une.edu
University of New South Wales; http://www.unsw.edu.au
University of Ottawa; http://www.uottawa.ca
University of Pécs; http://www.ki.pte.hu/
University of Queensland; http://www.uq.edu.au
University of South Africa; http://www.unisa.ac.za/
University of Stellenbosch; http://www/sun.ac.za/
University of Surrey; http://www.surrey.ac.uk/
University of Tampere; http://www.uta.fi/
University of Texas at Arlington; http://www.uta.edu
University of Texas at Austin; http://www.utexas.edu
University of Texas at Dallas; http://www.utdallas.edu/
University of Texas at El Paso; http://www.utep.edu
University of the Witwatersrand; http://www.wits.ac.za/
University of Turku; http://www.utu.fi/
University of Vaasa; http://www.uwasa.fi/
University of Vienna / Universität Wien; http://www.univie.ac.at/
University of Warwick; http://www2.warwick.ac.uk/
University of Washington; http://www.washington.edu
University of Western Sydney; http://www.uws.edu.au
University of Wisconsin; http://www4.uwm.edu/
University of Zagreb; http://www.unizg.hr/
Univerzita Konštantína Filozofa v Nitre/Constantine The Philosopher
    University in Nitra; http://www.ukf.sk/

Uniwersytet Im. Adama Mickiewicza W Posnaniu/Adam Mickiewicz University; http://www.guide.amu.edu.pl/

Uniwersytet Jagiellonski/Jagiellonian University; http://www.uj.edu.pl/

Uniwersytet Łódzki/University of Lodz; http://www.uni.lodz.pl/

Uniwersytetu Warszawskiego / University of Warsaw; http://www.ils.uw.edu.pl/

Wake Forest University; http://lrc.wfu.edu/

Washington Academy of Languages; http://www.wal.org

Western Michigan University; http://www.wmich.edu

Wright Sate University; http://www.wright.edu

Index

213

About the Author

Carline Férailleur-Dumoulin is the founder and President of CF Professional Translations, LLC. She holds a Bachelors Degree in Economics from Florida International University and a Certificate in General Translations from New York University. She is a member in good standing of the American Translators Association (ATA) and of the American Council on the Teaching of Foreign Languages (ACTFL). She has over 13 years of experience in language translations. She taught a Spanish translation course at Queens College in New York, managed the Translation Department of a private translation company in Manhattan for close to 2 years, and has 10 years of experience in the banking industry in administration, operations, customer relations and international departments. Ms. Dumoulin is also a Language Test Evaluator for several translation companies in the United States. Furthermore, she has worked abroad in India, Haiti, Jamaica, Puerto Rico and the Dominican Republic. She is fluent in English, French, Haitian Creole, and Spanish. She has been a guest speaker on blog talk radio with Anthony "Spark Plug" Thomas, the founder and publisher of *People You Need to Know*, an Atlanta-based business publication. Her company is featured in the 2009 Edition of *People you Need to Know* magazine, and has also been featured in the 2007 and 2008 Editions. Carline has always had a passion for languages, ever since her adolescent years and she looks forward to her many more valuable years in the language and translation industry.

Made in the USA
Lexington, KY
25 January 2011